William Dudley Pelley

Prologue

William Dudley Pelley (March 12, 1890 – June 30, 1965) was an American writer, spiritualist and political activist. He came to prominence as a writer, winning two O. Henry Awards and penning screenplays for Hollywood films. His 1929 essay "Seven Minutes in Eternity" marked a turning point in Pelley's career, earning a major response in The American Magazine where it was published as a popular example of what would later be called a near-death experience.

In May 1928, Pelley gained notoriety when he claimed he had an out-of-body experience in which he travelled to other planes of existence devoid of corporeal souls. He described his experience in an article titled "My Seven Minutes in Eternity", published in book form in 1933 as Seven Minutes in Eternity: With the Aftermath, originally probably appearing in The American Magazine in the late 1920s. In later writings, he described the experience as "hypo-dimensional". He wrote that during this event, he met with God and Jesus, who instructed him to undertake the spiritual transformation of America. He later claimed that the experience gave him the ability to levitate, see through walls, and have out-of-body experiences at will.

Pelley's belief is what he called "Soulcraft". Soulcraft is according to him the study of the great cosmic principles on which the universe is run; the mystical history of Man on this planet; the significance of the Great Avatar, Christ, in human destiny; the fundamental principle of the deathlessness of the human soul and human personality; the program by which each soul is permitted to experience as many mortal lives as it desires for the

Star Guest ..
Design for Morality

By

William Dudley Pelley

SAUCERIAN PUBLISHER
Original Sources in Ufology

ISBN:**978-1-955087-34-6**

© 2022, Saucerian Publisher

Al rights reserved. No part of this publication maybe reproduced, translate, store in a retrieval system, or transmitted in any form or by any means, electronic, mechanical, photocopying, recording or otherwise, without prior written permision from the publisher.

perfection of its celestial character; and the enigmas of eternity that puzzle the orthodox Christian whose spiritual horizons are bound by the so-called Plan of Salvation. It neither contradicts nor combats orthodoxy but develops out of it and beyond it. Soulcraft has no denomination, no political slants, no surreptitious axes to grind, no other motive behind its tenets than to aid distraught people desiring more nourishing spiritual food than conventional forms of religion may furnish them.

He died on June, 1965, and left a set of twelve volumes, each containing 13 lectures (making a total of 156), which is called The Soulcraft Scripts. Each of these lectures is made up of a direct message received by Mr. Pelley from Mentor Minds on the Other Side of Life, together with his own comments and interpretations with an appropriate Master Message [Elder Brother] added. Each of these Scripts may be read by itself with much to be gained, although it is true that more will be gained by reading the later after the earlier. \

Saucerian Publisher was founded with the mission of promoting books in Science Fiction. Our vision is to preserve the legacy of literary history by reprint editions of books which have already been exhausted or are difficult to obtain. Our goal is to help readers, educators and researchers by bringing back original publications that are difficult to find at reasonable price, while preserving the legacy of universal knowledge. This book is an authentic reproduction of the original printed text in shades of gray and may contain minor errors. Despite the fact that we have attempted to accurately maintain the integrity of the original work, the present reproduction may have minor errors beyond our control like: missing and blurred pages, poor pictures and markings. Because this book is culturally important, we have made available as part of our commitment to protect, preserve and promote knowledge in the world. his title was originally published in 1950 and the present reprint once belonged to the former Cosmon Research Center (Solar Light Retreat) library founded by Aleuti Francesca.

The Solar Light Retreat was established in 1966 in the foothills in southern Oregon, 20 miles outside of Medford. Francesca (known initially as Marianne Francis; she changed her name legally in 1975) became interested in UFOs in 1947 in London, England, where she was born and grew up. In 1954 Francesca moved with her American husband, Kenneth Kellar, to Santa Barbara, California, where she also studied Hatha Yoga with Indra Devi and Baala Krishna. Telepathic and highly sensitive all her life, her sensitivity increased as she and Kenneth Kellar conducted experiments with Light Beam apparatus aimed at contacting outer space intelligences.

> Editor
> Saucerian Publisher, 2022

CONTENTS

To Resume	Page 9
What is Spirit?	47
Station-Stop Planets	71
The Great Abomination	93
Salvation Makes Sense	105
The Rage of Felines	113
On into Wisdom	125
Where Doctrine Came From	137
Discarding Fear	147
More About Earthly Return	171
The Elder Brother	191
If I But Gave the Word	199
The Goodly Company	213
The Christ Force	223
Grasping the Infinite	231
The Ancient of Days	247
The Second Coming	261
A Talk in a Garden	275
Divine Drama	291
Human Destiny	304
Benediction	315

TO RESUME

EARS ago it was, to be exact the 28th day of October, 1928, about nine o'clock in the evening. I sat on a divan in a sumptuous New York flat beside a middle-aged lady. The flat was located in the West Fifties and the lady was one of the leading editresses of Manhattan. It was her personal apartment where she lived with a colored maid and I was her author-guest for the evening, having arrived in town that afternoon from my then-residence in California. We sat side by side on the divan, I upon her right, and across our two laps lay a four-foot writing board. On the board was a pad of legal-sized writing paper. The right cuff of my hostess's housecoat was turned back

so I could lightly clasp her wrist, and held in her fingers was a vertical pencil. This pencil was writing.

The pencil was writing, I say, not the lady. That was the strange part. The lady was lying back relaxed, part of the time with her eyes closed, letting the pencil perform as it would.

The pencil was performing by writing word on word in intelligible composition. True, the words were strung together and when the end of a line was reached, a long slurring scratch made connection with the next line, but the writing was unmistakable. One might say at a glance that the lady was merely writing without looking at her penmanship but I was in a position to know differently. My left hand was clasping her right wrist, I say, my forearm flexed sufficiently to give her writing hand play. Who better than I was in a position to realize that my feminine friend wasn't driving her hand by muscular reflexes from her brain, but that my own hand was being motivated to travel synchronized with hers?

And this, literally, was the intelligence the spontaneous pencil was transcribing—

EMORY is not Memory if we must forever make new Thought-Bodies each time we give up our material bodies. Man will someday know the truth and then he will make new new bodies in the image of God. Make no mistake, we are those now in the Light and we have much to tell you. 'Music of the Spheres' is no idle phrase, but the center of the mystery of this, our universe.

"Where there is harmony there is life, and all discord is death. We of the more harmonious planes, which are next above the planes of earth, make this statement to you because you are of that company whose bodies are yet of earth but whose eyes are opened to perception of the truth.

"Many of us are with you, not alone at this moment but in many moments when you are unaware of our presences. We will make more power for you in all that you undertake if you will but open yourselves more completely to our touch . . "

This was my first experience with what I later heard called Clairaudient Writing or psychical intercourse. I had never experienced anything like it before and was intellectually uneasy. Hadn't Mary written it from her subconscious? Why not? It looked easy enough to write. All one needed to do, apparently, was master the technique of making a pencil operate without watching it. I said some such thing.

"I know," Mary smiled. "Only, what makes the words appear to me mentally before the pencil records them, and how do I record them with your left hand holding back my wrist?"

"Holding it back!" I exclaimed. "I wasn't holding it back. I was letting my hand go wherever yours went."

¶"Uh-huh,.. and my sensation was letting my hand go wherever yours went. I seemed to follow your lead with my hand as my feet might yours in a dance."

¶"Do you mean to imply that I wrote this syllogism, subconsciously or any other way, using your hand to transcribe it?"

"I can imply it," she contended, "just as logically as you can imply that I wrote it with my eyes shut. However, I'll tell you this: I have reasons for accepting that neither of us wrote it, or rather, that neither of us composed it. Let's say for tonight that it was composed by Invisible Intellects, motivating the hands of both of us to transcribe it."

"Invisible Intellects!" I remember exclaiming. "You mean spooks?"

She smiled again—tolerantly. "Illiterate people might refer to them as spooks. Those of us who've done considerable research in such matters, have satisfied ourselves there's such a thing as Discarnate Intelligence, and that's a nicer term for them. Remember what the astronomer and psychical scientist, Flammarion, said."

¶ "What did he say?" I inquired.

"After investigating the phenomena in three hundred and seventy-six haunted houses in France and writing his book 'Haunted Houses' in report on them, he concluded with a statement that went something like this: 'I'm persuaded that there exists in nature, in myriad activity, a psychic element the essential nature of which is still hidden to us'."

"All right, Flammarion said that, but what does it go to prove?"

"It goes to prove nothing," conceded my companion, "but it does attest that some mighty sound and well-grounded brains have delved into the phenomenon of Discarnate Intelligence and come to the conclusion that it exists and performs. To shut our minds to it, or the possibility of it, accomplishes nothing but forgoing the wisdom that might be rendered available to us—and does become available to us—as we credit its validity and permit it cooperative exercise."

"And this is a sample of it?"

"This is a demonstration for your skeptical benefit of one aspect of its operation."

"I've got to have more proof than this, Mary, before I can accept it as uncontestable truth."

"All right, I'll experiment for you—or we'll experiment together during your stay here in New York—and see how you feel about it before your time comes to leave."

¶ "Experiment how?"

"I'll give the whole coming fortnight to you, at least in

my evenings if you'll come up. If the pencil I hold begins to record intelligence that simply couldn't be produced by either of our subconscious minds, you'll be forced to concede that some third intelligence is at work. Right?"

"But what couldn't be produced by our subconscious minds?"

"That's a rather ridiculous question, isn't it? There's a plethora of information for which we might ask .. about the great mystical premises of Nature and Life .. that can't be in our subconscious minds because the answers aren't known."

"You're telling me we might secure such information?"

"We can continue to write experimentally like this, and see what we do get."

"Well, .. if it means coming up to this charming apartment night after night and holding your lovely hand, I'm not disposed to fight it."

"Come up tomorrow night and we'll try it again at any rate. You're not erudite enough in all this as yet to appreciate what a psychic battery for this sort of thing you are, yourself. Forget my lovely hand. Concentrate on the Pencil."

N OCTOBER 29th I appeared at the flat on schedule. When we had prepared the lap-board and gotten ourselves settled for a long evening of such writing, the Pencil started to "act up" anew. This is what it wrote: "Many are the ways by which we approach those we are to help. Many of your most important acts are motivated by us. We are often able to make an impression on you when you least suspect our presences. We are in the very cores of your hearts, so to speak, and from there we direct your thoughts as the circulation of the blood proceeds from that organ. We are in your very midst and all you need do is to unbolt the door to

"Memory is the very essence of what you know as life. We know that Memory is but one phase of life and the more vital aspects of living are in the creation of new memories that shall in turn be replaced by others. We are of particular value to you in this, because the new memories must be finer and more beautiful than those which you are constantly outgrowing.

"Many are the lessons of adversity and few there are who find their true meaning and are ready to pass on to new lessons based on the life of the Spirit."

The rest of the message we took that evening belongs elsewhere, but the next night we transcribed a preachment on Art—which definitely convinced me we were not projecting this material subconsciously—

NOT theology but Art," the Discarnate Intelligence transcribed promptly, "is the very handmaiden of God, and the chosen priesthood of the temple is not recruited from any clergy in frocks so much as from the ranks of artists clad in the humble smocks that are the mark of their craftsmanship. Not that the painter only is the priest. We liked that figure of speech and so made one branch of Art stand for all the rest.

"No matter how far man may go along his destined path of evolution, the artist in imagination may still blaze the trail that the world of men will follow, with the scientist well toward the rear and the theologian struggling along in the dust-cloud. This does not include all scientists nor all theologians; occasionally one of them is an artist, and just so far as he is an artist, he is a force for the Good that he preaches, or the knowledge with which he would enlighten the world.

"Art is the greatest of all the mysteries!

"As we have no formula for the creation of the thing we call Life, so we have no hallowed definition for the thing we call Art. Words are only symbols, and when you apply them to the Eternal Verities, they become only symbols of the limitation of the human concept. So Art is to each man the highest good he is able to conceive, the deepest beauty he is able to perceive, in whatever aspect of Man, Nature, or God, he is at the moment considering! If his concept is in its essence true, if his perception is in its essence accurate, then he has what we call the 'creative instinct' and the thing which he produces is worthy to be dignified with the title of Art.

"Only remember: that there may be Art in the simplest act of the humblest creature's day. Art is a spirit and they who worship her must worship her in spirit and in truth. Many of the greatest artists have shut their hearts to her, because they considered her price was too great to pay. They did not know that the only price was relinquishing the bonds of limitation and that only by paying the price could they taste the very joys for which they refused it."

NOW to show you how one may go from point to point in this sort of thing until exploring its profundities becomes one of life's major activities, on the fourth night of the uncanny converse I began asking questions. If subconscious mind propounded the intelligence, what would be its reactions to inquiries on practical matters? And was it permissible to put them if Discarnate Intelligence of some sort was expressing the sentiments and not our own blind thinking at all? The answer came back—

"No, we think you should solve such problems for yourselves in the light of what we tell you, both through the medium of this Pencil and by means of direct impressions on your minds. We can only help you when you are in a quiet and relaxed state, which you have not been in the past. This fact has established certain habits of strain that have not fully left you. Many of the questions that puzzle you are of such a nature that it is only when you have 'grown up', psychically speaking, that we can answer them—and you will be able by that time to supply the answers yourselves. We will try, however, to give you some suggestions as to the meaning of your hyperdimensional experience which you recently wrote up for The American Magazine under the title, 'My Seven Minutes in Eternity' and which you mentioned earlier this evening in our hearing. This was not strictly a personal matter but one of the experiences that come to certain people, of vital significance to this kind of phenomena and contact. We are able to get to you now much better because your consciousness was able to come to us as it did, for even so fleeting a moment . . "

A more or less hard-shelled newspaperman and magazine writer, I had undergone a queer psychical transition one night in May of that current year, in which it seemed to me that I had vacated my body and "visited" individuals in a subliminal location, who by all mortal standards were assumed to be dead. The experience had simply happened to me, I had neither sought nor induced it deliberately. And it had puzzled and disturbed me. The article I subsequently wrote about it has been so widely published and quoted that description of it here is superfluous. But this night, with recollection of my experience so graphic in my memory, I was prompted to ask—

"What was the import of a certain woman's being with those whom I encountered in a discarnate state that night, whom I later found to be alive physically?"

The answer was: "We are not at all certain of the meaning of her presence, but we are of the opinion that what you perceived, or confronted, among the groups of real people, was merely a Thought-Form which you yourself projected. We have heard you state to your present companion that this particular person appeared not to have eyes, that you could look directly through the orifices of her face as through a mask, whereas the others whom you confronted had every semblance of reality. This would further bear out the explanation that she was a Pattern Creature of your own design."

¶ "Did I actually DIE that night?" I asked anxiously.

¶ "Not exactly," came the answer. "When you die actually—there is no such thing, of course—but when you come up into our more radiant dimension to stay for your allotted period on the next stage of your life's journey, you cannot go back. In all other aspects you did what you call 'dying' . .

"I wish," I said to Mary, "I might have stayed in that Discarnate State, in order to have done with this world of troublesome reality."

"Oh no, you don't!" the Pencil wrote swiftly. "You didn't want to come back at the moment because you had caught a glimpse of the beauty of the world of spirit. But if you came to us now and left your work unfinished in the vineyard of the earth, you would be selfishly shirking the thing you must do, and you would find yourself serving a long probation before you achieved again the beauty that was yours for that transcendent sojourn."

"I didn't mean," I hastened to say, "that I wanted to commit a sort of suicide in order to make the experience permanent."

"We know your meaning more than you know yourself," the Intelligence responded promptly, "because it concerns the innermost center of your personality with which we are in touch. There is, in every human heart, a hunger for the things of the Spirit, but in many this desire has become so embalmed with the poisons of the purely fleshly desires that for all practical purposes it no longer exists. This does not mean a denial of the desires of the flesh that are a legitimate part of all spirit-growth. Growth lies in accepting the flesh in which you pass through this mortal stage of your spiritual education. Live in it and through it, until you have made it the radiant garment through which all men see the glory of the Spirit shine.

"There is no conflict between flesh and spirit. They are of one substance. It is only when Flesh has fallen from its high estate that it becomes the foe of spiritual manifestation."

ROUGHT up in orthodoxy as I had been, this was electric intelligence .. if it truly came from persons in more sublime dimensions who knew what they were talking about. "Does this last assertion," I inquired, "refer to physical dissipation or the incorrect use of the physical assets to material pursuits?"

"All of the last and more. The Mind, and the Spirit that uses Mind as an instrument, are able to change the flesh to their needs but only when they are recognized as the supreme authority. When flesh dominates, then has it fallen from its high estate of service and is prostituted indeed. But .. better a night of dissipation than a moment of hatred. Better a complete life of self-indulgence and eating and drinking, than an uncharitable judgment of one of whose inner struggles you can have no knowledge. The so-called 'Sins of the Flesh' do not exist excepting as they are symbols of utter spiritual failure!"

B SAID: "Then people really do a lot of unnecessary worrying over Sins of the Flesh, it appears?"

"There is no growth," the Pencil replied, "excepting as we learn the true meaning of Love. Love has an infinite number of forms but it is never love unless it finds expression. By expression we mean, externalization of the Inner Motive. That is, by its fruits ye shall know the tree .. old and yet just as true as when it was first expressed."

I was beginning to be convinced, as one has to be convinced, that this sort of thing wasn't originating in either Mary's or my subconscious mind, entirely aside from the mechanical difficulties that would have been involved in both of us agreeing spontaneously on the thought to be transcribed. Mary and I were both "good haters" in our personal likes and dislikes of certain individuals who had a propensity for getting in our hair. We would scarcely do an about-face and preach sweetness and light from our subconscious minds just because we were in contact and writing thus necromantically. I observed—

"How relieving to receive Instruction that comprises something besides a dour list of Thou-Shalt-Nots!"

"Thou-Shalt-Nots," the Pencil picked up reactively, "are for those in the childhood of the race that can see little in the universe beyond the fences of the father's yard. We who have outgrown them must not make the mistake of thinking that the children would be morally safe without them. We are making a very great effort to graduate a few of your generation onto the Advanced Planes, and some of you are showing ability which gives us hope that we may make monitors of you. We are, for this reason, taking rather personal charge of your education, and we hope that we shall be able to do this increasingly as you grow in understanding of what you are to do."

"This is all like coming out of darkness into a great light!" I exclaimed.

"THERE is no darkness," the answer came, "excepting as you close your eyes to light. Love is a vibration of an infinitely higher rate than any known to your present world of science, and it is therefore able to transmute and recreate all things that feel its power. There can be no limitation to this power. The limitations are only in the object that fails to make itself a vehicle for the power. So you must learn each day to open your hearts a little wider to love. You must learn each day a new way to give that love expression. As you grow in your ability to feel and to release love, so you will draw into yourselves more and more of the force that alone is able to give you contact with those of us who are upon This Side of the Road."

"How unusual," I remarked to Mary, "to have the

separation between the earthly and spiritual levels designated as a Road. We ordinarily think of it as a veil or a barrier."

"But there are no barriers in the universe of Truth! What seem barriers to you are but creations of fear that are the children of Hate and therefore the antithesis of Love. A Great Teacher has told you that 'love casteth out fear.' We say to you more than that. Where Love is, no fear can find entrance. When the sun is high in the heavens, how can there possibly be shadows?"

In the next sentence which our twin hands appeared to be writing unassisted, it seemed as though the Discarnate Intelligence were speaking in an aside from its dimension:

"Many of us are now drawn into your circle who have seen the light that surrounds it, and are come that they may learn of the Wise Ones who teach you. Now to resume—

"We may not give you more than the smallest glimpse of the mysteries that we may one day reveal to you. As you ponder in your hearts the words you have received, we shall breathe into them the breath of life and each one shall be unto you as an arrow that points the way to us. In the silence of your souls we will speak again, and when once we have this access to you, you will be ready for much that we must not now attempt to give you."

"That requires some patience on our parts," I said.

"Patience is one of the manifestations of Love, and without it spiritual development is impossible. Many a spiritual battle has been lost because the importance of patience was not fully understood. Patience has no kinship with Resignation. Patience is positive. Resignation is negative. Do you need further explanation of that truth?"

I said that we didn't.

"We are glad. We are giving you rather heavy doses because they are to be digested over a period of time when we must depend on fleeting impressions for our contacts with you."

"This type of instruction is like drinking from a fountain of pure cool water after years of torrid thirst."

"Yes—the Living Water indeed! There is no spiritual fault in ignorance unless it be willful ignorance. And even willful ignorance is the result of Fear, rarely the cause. We mean by Fear in this connection, the refusal to open the mind to knowledge because of the reaction of obligations recognized. Fear, you understand, is always buried beneath the threshold of Consciousness and is not always recognized for what it is."

I said, "To me the mystery of this whole interpretation is in the selection of one with such inadequate attainments as mine to receive it."

"We never waste our riches," our mentors responded, "nor do we throw our pearls before swine. Draw your own conclusions." Were our mentors smiling at that? "It all leaves me wondering how many times I've been discoursing with others, when my expressions mayn't have been my own at all, but contributions made to my discourse by these obviously Unseen Friends."

"Perhaps we did join in, more than you suspected. We are sure of you, else we never would have undertaken this work. Much, of course, hangs upon the meanings in words. When we thus try to reduce Truth to human forms which cannot be so confined, we must use the word that seems nearest to Truth and you must do the translating. However, we may help you in that as well, but it will only be when you are not conscious of the aid. May the seeds of this plant take firm root in the gardens of your hearts, so that they may one day afford shelter and sustenance to all who pass your way."

"How far," I asked, beginning by this fourth night to be "sold", but wondering what it meant for me, "how far am I to disseminate these truths in the literary form for the general public, seeing I'm privileged to have them given me?"

"YOU cannot go astray on that score," wrote the Miraculous Pencil, "because when you engage in that work we have easiest access to you. We are not literary critics and you may be allowed to commit blunders of craftsmanship, .. that part is YOUR job and you must find your help where in the past you have learned to seek it most profitably. But do not fear that our inspiration will fail you or that you will give out anything that is expressly for you at this stage of your enlightenment. We will make you worthy to be a preacher of this higher gospel if you will only perform at least one-half your share."

"Why suggest only one-half cooperation?"

"We merely make allowance for human limitation."

¶ "Then you can't hold a very flattering view of human limitation."

"We do, indeed! We have lived through human limitation ourselves and now we look on from the vantage-point of a world where Time, Space, and Matter are mere figures of speech. We must use YOUR terms when we reduce Thought to Form, and must seem therefore, for the moment, to have put on something of limitation ourselves. But take heart. You will be amazed at the speed with which you shed limitation, once you have embarked upon that journey that leads you into conscious realization of the Oneness of all life and the creative power of those vibrations that work through rhythm, harmony, and love."

E SAT thinking it over.

I said, "This only confirms what I've felt for some time: that all life is one essence, as the same sort of electricity lights the filaments of electric bulbs all over the world." ¶ "But don't forget," our mentors concluded, "that the humblest rock or stone are instinct with life in a lower vibration, that they are harmony and rhythm, and therefore Love, and therefore Life. All, we tell you, is motion. All is rhythmic motion. All is cosmic joy, excepting where the eyes are holden and will not see. We will give you no more of this converse tonight. Make the most of what has been transmitted and await with patience our pleasure . . "

The Pencil went dead . . and no amount of "taking thought" on Mary's and my part could reanimate it. Well, there it was.

I record these first conversations verbatim to give you an idea as to how I ever got started on this subliminal instruction. I did keep on coming up to Mary's apartment, writing so with her night upon night, until the date arrived finally when I was obliged to go back to my home in Pasadena. On November 1st we got instruction on the meaning of Humor. Maybe, before I proceed to tell how I altered my whole life-plan and gave myself over to publishing these books, I ought to reprint that so-called Humor message and its allied enlightenment, in order to give you, the reader, credence for the validity of the instruction with which this book deals.

After all, if you become convinced—as I became convinced—of the fact of Discarnate Intelligence, and by the same words and procedures, perhaps you can better understand what my program has been since. I had my own thinking on the mysteries of Cosmos so altered that I gave over my career to expounding these subjects publicly. That they landed me in a federal penitentiary was merely a repetition of all history for persons who attempt to bring humanity a new interpretation of the Truth

I have to report to you, in all sincerity and integrity, that starting from this session in Mary's New York apartment on October 28th, 1928, in the manner I have set down, I found ways of my own after returning to California to transcribe over ONE MILLION WORDS of information that I contend belongs only to the higher octaves of life..

"E ON the mortal side of life," I remarked this fifth night, when Mary and I were prepared to take the discourse, "do not mean to be disrespectful in any humorous reference we make to those in the Higher Octaves of existence merely because they're invisible to us. But this situation does have its humorous aspects."

Neither of us knew who our mentors were, of course. It might have made the situation still more ridiculous to us had we known. The intelligence we were recording had to stand or fall on its merits.

"Humor," the Intelligence proceeded to expound, "is another of the essential ingredients of Love. Love is made up of many elements and Humor is its harmonizer—the binding force that holds those elements together. Humor is an attribute of the spirit of God. Self-pity and scorn may be the motivations behind certain types of laughter but between laughter and humor may be a great gulf. The laughter that is of the essence of humor is as the laughter of the gods and no sound is more lovely in all the universe. Conversely, no sound is more hateful to the ear of Spirit than ribald mirth in which there is neither loving kindness nor tender mercy. Such mirth is to the sensitive ear as the hollow dropping of clods upon the coffin that holds the body of one who went out of earth-life in the darkness of fear and doubt . . "

"What a shock it might be to some sanctimonious persons," I remarked, "to think of Jesus telling a mirthful joke. Perhaps it was because of His very human qualities, creating or drinking wine and consorting with publicans and sinners, that the Pharisees hated Him."

"So it was in very truth. And so it is ever with those who come to give us a new and more beauteous interpretation of life."

"Then all this instruction sums up to a sort of adjuration to cease being glum and solemn over sacred subjects and try to be joyous and happy?"

"Yes, but there is no more difficult task in all the world, dear brother and sister."

"Why shouldn't we be happy, however, with such revelations as these to take away our unnatural inhibitions and puritanical repressions?"

"Ah, yes. But how many years of struggle and bitter pain must precede such realization?"

"Perhaps the moments of bitter pain had for a premise the realization of the hurt that our behavior was inflicting on others?"

"It does not matter what the cause of the pain. You must endure it and know it if you are to stretch your spiritual muscles, giving them the exercise that is essential to growth."

"Do Mary and I disturb you by pauses for comment between ourselves?"

"Quite the contrary. We are glad to have you discuss these problems and use your own minds."

"Sometimes such confirmation of things we've long suspected but scarcely dared hope to be true, brings tears of emotion."

"Tears are but laughter attuned to the promptings of humility when shed in such a cause as this. In all real recognition of beauty, tears are the index of the recognition, whether they be shed from the eyes or from the heart. Where there is feeling there is the capacity for Love and its expression. Pity only those who have not shed the tears of exultation that cleanse and purge the soul. Why do you doubt us? If we thought you were wrong in yielding to your emotions, we would promptly preach self-control."

"What, by the way, is inhibition—as you see it from your higher vantage-point of observation?"

HEN the Mind and the Spirit are divorced and the Mind takes charge of the body, usurping the throne of its master—Spirit —the result is warfare between the mental and the physical. This is the state in which self-control degenerates into what modern psychology knows as Repression and Inhibition."

"But," I argued, "isn't Mind the substance—or at least the instrument—of Spirit? How can Mind alone take charge of the body as though it were a separate controlling entity in human affairs? Isn't it Spirit's agent?"

"Yes, but you can shut the Spirit out and eventually so plaster up the gates that only a miracle can open them. Whether you leave the gates open or closed is the meaning, and the only meaning, of the theological term Free Will. We are not making things more difficult than is usual when you try to reduce thoughts of Infinity to concrete terms of mortality. When the gate to Spirit is closed, it is as though the ruler of a kingdom and all

the branches of government, claimed the supreme authority. Your own little personal spirit may keep the authority for a while but having been subordinate to the ruler it will sooner or later be overcome by the forces of Mind or Body. Only in contact with the Master lie wisdom and strength. Deprived of these it grows more and more futile until the day finally comes when it is buried under illness or mental disorder. Mental disorder means infinitely more, of course, than the world means by insanity. When the Mind assumes control, then the body rebels and the whole mechanism is in a state of turmoil whose outcome is illness or death, or the loss of the very power that has dared to take charge. There is no Frankenstein to be compared to the human mind when its master has been shut off from contact with Infinite Spirit that alone keeps the individual spirit alive."
¶ "But in all this differentiating between Mind and Spirit," I returned, "will you not explain just what is first meant by Mind as distinguished from Spirit on the one hand and physical brain on the other?"

IRST," these Invisible Teachers complied, "is the Universal Spirit from which all things proceed and which is of all things the substance. Next is the Spirit of the Group which animates all the lower forms of creation. When we come to Man, however, we have a new problem. There is now in each human soul a

separate and distinct development of the Universal Spirit which has a body for expression and which is yet able to be aware of its kinship with Divine Essence. There must be an instrument for this awareness, and this instrument is Mind. It acts upon the brain, and through the brain upon the body. If there is a break in this chain at any point, then the whole plan of creation is invalidated insofar as that individual is concerned. There is, however, no disaster so complete or so irremediable that it cannot be salvaged, except that break between individual and Universal Spirit. So long as the bond between these two holds, then all things are possible to the body and the mind through which Spirit speaks. So you see it is indeed the Unpardonable Sin and its 'unpardonableness' is automatic. Cut off from the source of Life and therefore isolated from the vibrations of Love, what can the wages be if they are not death? Indeed, that IS death!

"The problems of the world of matter in which you move therefore, are chiefly one problem. If you keep the bond unbroken and the gate of vibration open, you will receive all the Light, all the Understanding, all the Wisdom, you need. And remember that understanding is always the measure of forgiveness. To understand all is to forgive all, and when you pass judgment upon another soul, it is only to judge your own and disclose your own limitations."

"Where then," I inquired, "does Memory come in?"

"Memory of the past," our Miraculous Pencil wrote, "is not only memory of the present stream of your consciousness but of the history of your soul's growth from the beginning of its awareness of itself and of its mission. So when you judge another soul you must have intimate knowledge, not only of its struggles here and now but of the handicaps it has brought with it into its present incarnation."

"Incarnation! Incarnation and reincarnation are facts of life, then?"

"This incarnation means the one you are at present undergoing. Incarnation on your earth is for the purpose, as you say, of developing the individual consciousness to complete realization of itself and of its source. But surely you cannot think that this is to be accomplished in the short span of one little lifetime, even though it were twice as long as Methuselah's. No, that would be hard indeed on the little children who die in infancy. It would be Infant Damnation with a vengeance!"

ERE was food for the most profound thought. I realized that we people of the West looked on reincarnation as merely an eccentric doctrine originating in India for the purpose of explaining many facts of life that otherwise went unrationalized. Here were subliminal mentors apparently coming to us in a New York apartment, giving no evidence of being "East-

erners", speaking or writing excellent English, and treating of Re-Existence as though it were the most accepted of subjects in their psychology and logic. But I wanted to be sure of it ..

"If this instruction definitely postulates what is popularly known as reincarnation," I argued, "then would it not seem that projection from the Thought Plane back to a material world would be a form of retrogression?"

"There is no retrograde in the development of the spiritual individuality," came the answer. "But there must be, between the pain of each incursion into lower and more atomic matter, a period of rest and refreshment upon the so-called Planes of Thought. Here the lessons of each mortal life are reviewed in the full memory of the entire soul history. When you go back—that is, into Earth-Life—you do so at the recommendation of those who no longer are obliged to go back and yet are passing up for a moment in eternity the bliss of going on to higher realms of spirit, that they may be missionaries upon the Planes of the Invisible. It is they who help you. It is they who aid you to discover and determine the moment and the place that shall make your coming earth-visit possible in profit. That is, they advise you and assist you in the decision so that you may learn what lesson you still need most, and so make your repeat visits as few as possible in number. Make no mistake here, we speak whereof we know! When you say 'I had it coming to me!' you speak more profoundly than you realize. We are now making an effort to teach you some of the truths which, if you enter into them and come to know them as accepted conclusions in your thinking, may save you more than one of the earthly sojourns that are ahead for you otherwise

"This cycle of earthly revisitation goes on until its glorious culmination in its recognition of its unity with Universal Spirit."

"Then this process means practically a constant oscillation between the Earth-Plane and the Thought-Plane, doesn't it?"

"Yes, but with an ever-upward swing. The cycle is interrupted only when the spirit loses touch with Love, as we have previously narrated to you. Then follows the only death there is. The individual consciousness loses awareness of its own nature and lapses back into the Eternal Ocean of Spirit, no longer a separate drop which is part of the whole, but completely merged and with individuality destroyed. This death may be coincidental with the body's or it may precede that event by years!"

"But I seem to discern a certain selfishness," I said, "in such an oscillation, using a world of other souls as a sort of ladder for one's own development."

"You are so using it. But the Great Master has told you the secret. Only he who loses his life in loving service for others shall find it. That life exists at all is a paradox and you can never understand its inner meaning until you have meditated upon, and pondered in your hearts, those lesser paradoxes that have their origin in the heart of the Great Mystery of Life. Do you go your pathways, wherever they may lead you, sure and calm and free. We are beside you, and so long as you hear our voices in your hearts, you cannot fail, no matter how rough or repellent the journey. No more tonight."

The Pencil stopped performing, and try as we would we could not restart it excepting by conscious muscular effort—which was commonplace literary composition of our known manufacture. A certain something that I might best describe as "the vibration of a Presence" seemed to have departed our vicinity. However, we had enough—or at least I had enough—to make me do some epochal thinking. I had been thirty-eight or more years living a layman's life by orthodox thought-processes and attaining, as I considered, no little success in it. But here were communications commanding respect. I jogged up Mary's many sheets on which all of the foregoing had been written, and with her gracious permission stored them in my pocket for subsequent copying. It has been from the copies made the next day that I have borrowed the preachments that are the substance of this chapter.

It is one thing, I find, to receive the fundamentals of a doctrine from another through the medium of his personal interpretations—strained through the personality and intellect, so to speak—and quite another to learn of those fundamentals precisely as he learned them.

For this doctrine, begun under the conditions and auspices I have narrated, was to change my whole life and shape my entire career. Before another week of such transcription had passed, long before I was ready to return to California, I was honestly convinced that Mary's and my subconscious minds had been concerned in no part of the intelligence we had written. And my reasons for concluding so were these—

We were getting material, and examples of ideas, that by no means could have found lodgment in our minds before the present. This was particularly demonstrated to me weeks and months later when I began taking a series of papers on Embryology. I had never read up on Embryology and neither had my woman companion of that later period. Especially we had never acquainted our minds with the technical and physiological terms with which one must be familiar to understand that subject. When the Pencil wrote of scientific terms that had never been in our subconscious minds, the conclusion was rational that they must have had origin in a source outside ourselves. The contention of modern psychology is, that one can never produce from the subconscious what has never gone into it.

Those fraught nights in Mary's apartment around the first of November, 1928, introduced me to a program of erudition that was impossible to ignore, I say. Returning in due course to southern California, I made a succeeding discovery. When I provided myself with a suitable feminine companion—to supply some species of psychical polarity—and took the Miraculous Pencil in my own hand, its performance was similar to my New York experience when Mary held it. I was the one who started "seeing the pictures of words" mentally, which the graphite subsequently reproduced upon paper.

I had written such subliminal material for three weeks to a month—in which most of my orthodox spiritual quandaries were being answered or dissolved, when I made the discovery that I had only to speak the words orally that I saw mentally, and have a stenographer take them in shorthand. Filling quires of legal-sized paper with pencil scrawls was merely a waste of good paper. I began "talking off" what came to me first in word pictures, and could not distinguish any loss of quality in the text. Thus I became adept in what is known as Clairaudience

It wasn't a matter of "hearing voices" which the uninitiated assume, and which the kitchen-garden variety of psychologist pronounces mental aberration. It is a matter of having a visual mind for words, a vocabulary more or less trained to depict ideas in adequate and skillful literary form, and more than all else the tacit presence of discarnate intellects with the willingness to transmit the erudition of their transcendent minds in such shape that it registers. And the last is the most essential. Without bona fide mentor being present, the result is mere subconscious fabrication.

For upwards of twenty-two years now, I have been employing such clairaudient faculties, I declare, in which time I have transcribed over ONE MILLION WORDS upon every spiritual and cosmic subject under the sun. A hundred thousand of that million I have published—up to this date in 1950 when this present volume is of moment. But I have scarcely scratched the surface of what remains to be published.

However, the fundamentals of what "invisible intelligences" passed down to me, commencing with those evenings in Mary's apartment, have long since been given out in the Sixty-Seven Scripts of the Liberation Assemblies, and the books "Behold Life", "Thinking Alive", "Earth Comes" and the "Golden Scripts". Now we come to a specific delineation of that most intriguing of subjects: How life in the human form made its advent upon the planet Earth. Let's keep as closely as possible to these first communications of mine, and receive the intelligence in the forms and phrases in which it was originally given. Glancing back across twenty-two years and perusing some of those first Scripts, I find the Mentor Papers more convincing than anything I might propound in exposition of them, despite the subsequent lore that accrued to me with the recording of a million additional words—when Clairaudience had become an accredited fact in my daily life and lost its first novelty. However, I should make this clear—

HERE did come a time in my later publishing program when I desired to copy and put in type some of these first communications, or the substance of them, for the books I was issuing. When I sat myself down in the privacy of my own study and began making transcripts of these first messages, "someone" seemed to come up behind me, as it were, and look over my shoulder. As I typed the original enlightenment on paper, I would have delineations and elaborations of certain truths supplied me, rounding out the diction and making the text more comprehensible or grammatical. Again and again this happened. For instance, much of the material quoted in this opening chapter I have already used on Pages 217 to 231 of "Thinking Alive". It seemed as though the Sages themselves had the desire to exercise a supervising eye on what was finally going publicly into type, and counseled me accordingly. As these delineations and interpolations did naught but enhance the original text, I by no means disregarded them. But I print the original text for the opening sequence of this present volume to acquaint thousands of new students to these doctrines with their genesis ✒

Again and again this sort of thing may be noted, not

only in this current work but in volumes to be forthcoming. I solemnly contend that I had no more to do with the corrections or additions than I had to do with the messages originally transcribed. However, I have of my own volition deleted constant personal references of no great public interest. Literality of text, I discovered subsequently, was by no means insisted upon by those giving me the material. "You are expected to be the craftsman on your side, and to your own mortal world," I was on one occasion advised. "If you make basic alterations in the doctrine, wittingly or unwittingly, we shall do what we can to prevent publication. But you are selected for this work because you do have the gift of literary expression, and making the wisdom interpretable and rational is expressly your responsibility."

Let me add but one word more about repetitions of messages. Sometimes the clairaudient expositions may appear in one form in one book, and in an enhanced form in another book, to prove higher confirmation of some subject under discussion. Do not be exercised by such occurrences. Remember that no message has ever been relayed to mortality that will not stand many republishings. But greater than that, not all who read the later volumes will have been fortunate enough to have had access to those first printed. Be generous with these new readers and give fresh attention to whatever republishings are made. Generally speaking, they will be held to a minimum. But sometimes a given communication delineates more than one point of basic doctrine, and different phases are accentuated. Take all these volumes in their stride and try to get the great general gist of what the Sages are attempting to propound ⚝

With this introduction for "Star Guests", let's talk for a time about the commencements of mortal life on this earth-ball and utilize such enlightenments further in the main library of Scripts as have a bearing on the subject.

WHAT IS SPIRIT?

WHAT IS SPIRIT?

IT SURPASSED all other thrills of life, at least to one of my temperament, to be able to ask any question occurring to me about the nature of Cosmos and have an answer returned that transcended my knowledge of the moment. I couldn't ask questions fast enough. I felt a renewal of that inquisitive childhood state I had known at the age of four when I had shocked my orthodox father by asking: "Daddy, if God can see everywhere and everything, can He see the back of His own head, and how does He do it?" Only these new mentors didn't adjure me to be more respectful, and besides, wasn't it long past my bedtime? Always a sincere attempt seemed being made to return me explanations to my most bedeviling perplexities. And infallibly I kept these explanatory transcripts to read and ponder at my leisure. For twenty-two years now I have been reading and pondering them, sharing them perchance with a hundred thousand people to whom my literature has come. And the end is not yet . . .

E ARE many," the Sages said, when Mary and I began our session for the sixth succeeding night, "and our Younger Brother is merely the one who helps in making the link between us." This had reference to the specific individual on the Invisible Plane who was relaying us the picture words. "We descend from Higher Levels of Attainment and we come only when we find the vibrations waiting, formed by the junction of your personalities . .

"We are the Masters, and those who come to each of you alone are personal friends, but not Masters of the Wisdom. What we say, we know. Much of what the friends say is the fruit of knowledge with a broader background than yours of earth but still far from absolute. When we speak, they also listen and learn. We are come from realms which they have not yet entered, and we delay our progress that we may return to give you the teachings usually reserved for those who have been freed of mortal sheathings. We alone are to be heard without question and without reservation. That is because we alone are of the Higher Company who have grown beyond the necessity for further visits to your mortal world and are therefore able to make real contact with Celestiality . .

"Yes, all other contacts must be only partial and not of the nature of ours. By the Spirit is meant that which is created and IS the universe—and all other manifestations in whatever phase they appear.

"There is no God in the sense in which the mortal theologian uses the term. But we are by no means proclaiming atheism. You must come to understand clearly that to name and personify Infinite Spirit would be to limit It . .

"The word 'God' is merely the attempt of the human spirit-mind to make contact with something it is incapable of grasping. Only when the Mind stands aside and the Spirit functions does the reality hidden behind words appear, or begin to emerge . .

"Deity, God, Father, Son, Holy Ghost, Christ, Buddha, are all answers to the human need for form and all are veils to those who truly see!

"You whose eyes are beginning to be opened must still use the terminology of your fellows, but let it always be with the clear vision of that which habit and custom in the use of words may tend to blur for you . .

"When you say 'God', think always Spirit. When you say 'Christ', think always of Spirit made for the moment manifest. And so with those other incarnations of Spirit that have been masters and teachers of the race up the multiple generations . .

"Now we are come to our lesson of the evening. We are sure of you, and others on this side who are constantly in touch with you. We are able to come only when you are met for the purpose of receiving these teachings. The rest of the time we are about higher business. But be sure that we have reports on you from these friends who are so often with you. In all that concerns your earth-life we leave you to them. They are wise and faithful counsellors. but remember that when the stage of infallibity is reached, the entity is like unto ours and has no further contact with those matters that concern life on the plane of the physical. Trust those who guide you, but do not expect omnipotence nor omniscience. We are more nearly able to foretell the future than they are, but we are only interested in your growth into awareness of Spirit.

HERE there is Form there is difficulty in making clear a channel, no matter how much we all together try. And when the channel is not clear, there will be misinterpretation and confusion. It is easier to clear the channel for this teaching than for matters that concern your earth-lives because we are making a channel for the things of Spirit, and the emotions and desires of the body are not involved.

"As we have already written, there is one Law and one Force and one Harmony only in the universe, and that is Love. There is no other God but that one Law and Force and Harmony that is Love. There is no other master of the Spirit than that.

"When you are together and in harmony, then we can come to you either by writing through an intermediary or by direct impression upon your Inner Ear. It is only when you are together and sitting with such purpose in mind. We never come to you under any other circumstances, as our particular work is to get things to you as groups and we must have the synchronization that results from your physical contact. Physical contact means the electrical magnetism that plays between the positive and negative poles that are the male and female personalities. Your bodies do not have to be in actual contact but they must approach within a short distance of one another. We digress to mention such things because so many people who desire to receive such instruction directly are not always aware of the mechanics involved, and when they fail to get profitable results are prone to fabricate information from their own intellects without always being guilty of dishonesty. Now to return to our discourse . .

N the Beginning there was only Spirit, or the essence of self-aware and self-forming Thought, as in the end there will be only Spirit, and as at the present moment in the affairs of the universe there is only Spirit. Out of Spirit, made Matter for purposes of Love by vibration, was formed the solar universe with which you are most familiar and many a universe afar from you, some of which have not as yet been located by your astronomers' telescopes.

"Each universe has its own kind of life, its own method of growth, and its own character development, but all have the one objective, difficult as it is for your mortal and finite minds to encompass: that 'far-off divine event toward which all creation moves' although the poet little understood the magnitude of the occurrence of which he wrote. It is the final union of each particle of Spirit with that Master Spirit from which it came, only in the beginning of its separation into Form it was unconscious of its nature, its career, and its high destiny . . . Through interminable ages it clothes itself in ever more complex form. Through interminable ages it grows more and more intricate and adds to itself more duties and functions until it has progressed from what is called the inorganic to organic matter. Now it is ready to know a sort of Cosmic Urge that links it to the life of the planet it is evolving upon. But it is not yet conscious of its own nature. Remember we are describing to you now the spirit-growth of people who are indigenous to a planet on which they find themselves maturing. We are not describing the growth of those souls known as the Sons of God who came to this planet to redeem the indigenous forms from Sodomy.

"This whole phenomenon of Self-Aware Thought, that brings all this through processes and into fruition, is the Spirit-Essence which you commonly picture to yourselves as God. You in your mortal encasements are so close to your own bodies, by the fact of your individual spirit's residence in them across the spans of your mortal lives, that you mistake the resident for the residence. You say you can't 'think' lacking a body and brain to perform the process of thinking. We tell you that Thought is a manifestation of Pure Spirit—the really Divine Spirit—and requires no protoplasmic mechanism. That is the basic marvel about Thought, and particularly Divine Thought, which for want of a better term man calls Holy Spirit, that it is self-functioning, and out of it in its non-physical state comes all Matter and all Substance and all Protoplasm, being the author and creator of these in the atomic and material sense

"This has been the meaning of the first two verses of the first chapter of Genesis, 'In the Beginning God created the heaven and the earth. And the earth was without form, and void, and darkness was upon the face of the deep; and the Spirit of God moved upon the face of the waters'. . . . Self-aware Thought requires no medium but itself—in other words—in order to achieve performance. It is a principle of the universe, just as atomic material is another principle of the universe—when the first principle has brought the second principle into existence.

"It is by no means begging the issue to say that Thought thus thinking, of and by itself, is almost incomprehensible to your minds while encased in your protoplasmic selves. Divine Spirit is actually the phenomenon of it, that Thought can and does think without an organic mechanism, just as Light—or rather the vibrations that make for Light—can and does exist of itself whether or not there be organic eyes to behold the luminous properties of it or not. It is almost asking you to grasp a fourth-dimensional activity to propound this character of Thought and expect you to grasp it, just as it would be futile and meaningless to ask you to appreciate what luminous light was, if eyes had never been evolved

"God—or this ability of Thought to perform of Itself in a boundless universe—conceives and projects all that IS, and in this respect may be said to create all that is out of His own essence of Thought Performance.

"Looked at in another light, we may even put it that the material universe and all that exists within it of a material nature, partake of the literal composition of God. Even we in our spirits also partake of that literal composition in what we might term an animate expression. But that happens long after we have become conscious of ourselves as animate or organically housed entities 🙵

THE NEXT step upward is into the lowest and simplest forms of animate life. This is in the kingdom of what you call the vegetable. Next in the journey comes a feeling of dim and scarcely understood unity of all of Nature's forces. In the early striving of the Spirit Particle upward, a brooding Over-Spirit gives help and direction.

"When the Spirit Particle has finally worked its way up through the age-long procession of forms to the point of self-awareness, and yet has not evolved the mechanism of logicizing, we have the higher animals under the protection of the Group Spirit.

"This Group Spirit, so to speak, does their logicizing for them. For this reason we have the seemingly inexplicable instincts, such as the migrations of the birds, the hibernation of certain beasts, and the affinity of certain species for favorable localities to assure existence. For long ages this planet was the home of such animal life, strictly under the logicizing direction of Group Spirits, still another segmentary aspect of Holy Spirit's attaining to a desired result. Now listen carefully, for herein is a great truth and a great mystery—

"One group of those in existence in another planetary system that had gone farther than the group-logicizing animal systems, no longer depended solely on the latter but migrated through interstellar space and began to struggle independently with the problems of earth-planet environment.

"At that moment the Word was made flesh and man in his present form WAS!"

HIS, I realized, watching this discourse being written on Mary's pad, was the same thing as saying that Man in the form in which we know him did not originate on this planet, but I did not interrupt to challenge the instruction. Later I was glad I hadn't, as I shall point out in its proper place. I was to discover, far, far along in the Wisdom, that the Missing Link of the biologists, between the great apes and man, was a spiritual and not an organic Missing Link. Something or someone—or a great many someones—arrived on this earth-planet in the development of evolution, and incarnated in certain animal forms, causing the difference between the human and primate species. The primate species went on living and breeding as a true species, giving us the monkeys, apes, and gorillas of today. But those ape-forms that were borrowed for incarnation by the spirit-souls arriving from other areas of Time and Space, apparently supplied the original ex-

pressions of the human—which continued to breed and develop, and gradually sublimate the ape-forms into the races of man as society now recognizes them. More of this later . .

OW each man was an individual," the sages went on writing, "low in stature as in soul, but still Man. And as Man he began to feel dimly and fitfully a nameless longing for the spiritual home from which so many long eons before he had started out on this cosmic journey.

"Out of this longing he built his faith in gods!

"Out of this longing he built his desire for progress!

"Even in the days of his own Group Spirit on more distant star systems, he had known there was no going back to that from which he had originally come. He must advance or perish even from the ape-form he had achieved in this, his new home, or return to Matter in the earliest dust of the universe.

"Through all of this process there was only one motive: the desire of Infinite Spirit to share with each evolving particle the joys of Thought Creation. Instead of creating at one stroke a developed and fully conscious universe, there was given to EACH SPIRIT the joy of creating his own form and his own consciousness of his nature ⚹

"When man had become conscious of himself as a

thinking entity, though dimly, he was still not free from need of help from the Group Spirit, and at this time he developed a sense of kinship with Infinite Spirit which his advancing intelligence gradually made him question and then lose.

"But this was all a part of the Plan. If he had not lost his sense of dependence upon the Group and then upon Infinite Spirit, he would never have developed the Mind that must be a part of the mechanism of Man, who is in the highest sense aware of himself and Cosmos.

"Hence to the heart of the mystery . . .

S EACH Spirit Particle achieves manhood, it is exposed to temptations and it is given opportunities. As it responds to these tests is its next incarnation fixed and the "new" soul makes its real effort to live up to whatever dim and flickering light it has. As each soul makes its decision at each crossroads, that is, at each time of reincarnation, it has to abide by that decision and accept whatever is inherent in it. In this sense, all is foreordained. But within these limits the soul has choice that will affect its next incarnation. That is, even given the fixed elements that are the result of causes set in motion during earlier incarnations, you still have the power of choice whether you will go on in the next one to higher phases of life or whether you will close your eyes to the light and pay the penalty for it

in earthly sojourns still ahead down multiple careers. If from the beginning you were one of those who had closed his eyes, it shouldn't be hard to understand that many visits into fleshly form will be necessary to get a desire for light into the heart that has become inured to darkness.

"Many times a soul that has constantly chosen wrongly must go back to the earliest form of Man and join his brothers who are not far removed in consciousness from the early animal groups.

"The Group Spirit is not analagous to the individual entity; in fact, there is what corresponds to the Group Spirit in the special Order of Spirit (the Immortals) that is made up of the great teachers who have at one time or other manifested on the earth-plane and who are then placed in charge of various races with the Christ-Spirit over them all.

"In other words, Christ may be looked on as the Group Spirit for the mortal race upon this earth-planet. But now there must be conscious cooperation between Man and his Group Spirit in place of blind dependence as in the animal world.

"You ask if souls reincarnate from sex to sex. Some of them do and some of them do not. Those souls that have a full and complete growth, and have developed sufficient imagination and understanding—and often artistic ability—do not always need experience in both sexes. But those souls of narrow and restricted understanding and outlook must actually live in bodies of the opposite sexes in order to gain any understanding of their needs. To resume, however . .

HEN the individual entity begins his journey through the various incarnations in human form, he has a certain amount to learn before his graduation into Pure Spirit. His inheritance from a brute ancestry that is not exactly an animal ancestry—as you will learn in future—speaks through every phase of his spiritual development and equipment, and is unconsciously trying to draw him back into the unconsciousness of self-awareness from which he came. In his primitive forms he is not always able to distinguish between the Voice of the Spirit and the fears aroused by his own ignorance. Thus superstition is born and the pagan worship of symbols ⁂

"Life is a simple and straightforward proposition to these children of the early days of humanity, whether in prehistoric times or in the jungles of today. But even in the simplest organization of life there are those who strive to follow what little light they have, and there are those who close their eyes to that light and choose to dwell in darkness.

"Not even Infinite Spirit can explain why this choice is made in the beginning unless it be that in some physical organisms the Mark of the Beast—or the physical mechanism—is more vivid. That is, in the early struggle toward individual consciousness the traits of the animal ancestors are more strongly fixed upon one entity than upon another.

"In his first struggles with temptation the downward and backward pull is stronger upon him than upon his neighbor and his lower instincts more readily control him ☙

OW it should be plain that once having set the law of Cause and Effect in motion he must be more and more slow in his progress toward perfection and therefore require many more earthly careers before he reaches the spiritualized state, than the one who even in the beginning strove to overcome his bestial instincts and started to learn the meaning of Love.

"But do not think that this is an injustice. How many earthly careers are required, and how long each one is, is a matter of small consequence. The glory that is finally achieved is recompense enough, and even in the unhappiest earthly sojourn there are moments of delight in the earth, and in human contacts, that make it well worth having been endured. Now as to the problem of methods—

"Let us take one ordinary soul with the average number of successes and failures in resisting the temptations of its first earth-experience. We must remember that soul becomes Soul when the physical form of man has evolved, and the Mind and Brain are ready to function in such a way that the Spirit Particle is aware of itself as an individual entity, and henceforth its earth-lives—or earth-returns—are in its own keeping instead of in the keeping of the Group Spirit.

"Mind you, all of this is included in the answer to your question as to what Spirit is, and what the Divine Consciousness has evolved for the redemption and perfection of the individual Spirit Particle for ultimate reunion with Itself.

"After his passing from the earth-plane each time on physical death, the developing Spirit Particle is cared for on the Thought Planes and is there shown wherein it failed and sees what lessons it is still most in need of. In the earliest visits of man, the problem is extremely simple and he is usually told what he must do, and has little voice in it. This is particularly true of persons in the so-called 'savage' races. The further he travels into social complexity the more he is allowed to influence his incarnations. For this reason we can omit his earliest incursions into Matter and take him up at a point where some of his lessons have been thoroughly mastered. Having decided his needs, he begins a careful search through earth for the parents who can give him the environment he needs, and also supply him with the kind of body best suited to his manipulation.

"Thus is every man the spiritual son of the Spirit but

the physical son of the father and mother who bring him back for the period of the immediate life-cycle into the material universe. For example: say his lesson is to learn Patience. Then he chooses parents who pass on to him a highly sensitized and irritable nervous system over which, and through which, he can best learn self-control. In the physical body lies dormant all the racial and sodomic heritage, and thus we have those obscure and incomprehensible impingements upon spirit that the modern psychologist calls Complexes, Fixations and Neuroses.

ITH the progress of the soul through each earthly experience we are not now interested, but with the problem of the whole scheme of spirit in its earthly residence, bearing on what it is, and what its objectives. But mark this: when the soul starts upon its new career in flesh, it is naturally much closer to certain of its fellows than to others. By this we mean, the natural associations during its earlier earthly sojourns amid those who have been of one family or one neighborhood or those whose paths cross in such a way that Love or Friendship or Emnity are the result. In choosing the next environment on earth it is inevitable that many of those who were close to it should need pretty much the same lessons and should therefore choose bodies in the same environment, or even in the same families. As the

problem grows more complex and each soul has more widely varied experiences, this tends to be more broken up though it still continues to take place fairly often. But another element now enters into the situation—

"Two souls that have been very close but that have not made the same use of their opportunities, may find that one of them must have many more incarnations than the other. In such a case there have been instances where the more advanced one begged to take a longer time between his earth-lives that he might, from the invisible side, help the loved one. Thus they would be together in each of the advanced one's incarnations and would reach the end of their pilgrimage together. Thus those of you who have evidence of 'guardian angels' in your affairs, as you say, are really enjoying the help of someone who has been very close to you in lives past and therefore loves you and is maintaining an oversight over you that you may 'come out together' at the end of the Journey Beautiful. It is as simple as that.

"In lesser degree this applies to whole groups that have been together through some tremendous experience in some of the earlier earth-visits, and also to those unusually strong ties that are occasionally formed with a soul hitherto a stranger.

"With this as a background, do you not understand much that has been hidden? Do you not know the true meaning of much that has hitherto troubled and perplexed you?

HE AGE of the soul is not the important thing. What matters is its response to divine stimuli. There are those who must go through incarnations seventy times seven in order to know God. You ask why all do not make the same progress. You ought not to wonder at that, when you realize that all lives are not of the same environment and have different things with which to contend. You are to choose your own environment, perhaps, but all do not respond to that environment in exactly the same manner. The pity of all these earthly existences? Remember that not all are of your current sensibilities. Some do not want to tarry on the Thought Planes at all; they prefer to be in life, living according to the flesh. They are the 'beginners in living' who are to be pardoned for their lack of spirituality. They do not appreciate the joys of Pure Thought. They are the Unredeemed of the Bible who have no places to lay their heads.

"We shall tell you as much as we can about the Star Guests that all of us are, who came to this earth-planet upon an ancient time—and proceeded to appropriate the physical organisms of the primates for gradual spiritual evolution—but what we have had to say in this discourse has had chiefly for its substance the character and origin of spirit as spirit.

"There is in the universe, we say again, the essence of Self-Aware Consciousness that exists and persists in total independence of Matter. The nearest analogy we can make to it is Light. And yet it is more than Light, for Light itself is a component of its nature. It thinks and feels and exercises of, and to, itself and under certain conditions may formulate Matter by precipitating atoms. You must try to visualize such a Thought Essence in the abstract as you can, for by crediting it, or at least crediting the concept of it, you get explanation of many of the very material mysteries that perplex you ⚐

"Nothing from nothing, or nothing out of nothing, amounts to nothing, is true on any plane of reality. But Thought is not 'nothing' by any means—forgiving us the bad grammar. Thought, self-logicizing and self-analyzing, is the greatest and most dynamic Something that exists in all Cosmos and it behooves you to accept it for the present as prelude to expositions coming later that may make it much more clear to you.

"The way to go forward in this New Instruction—which is a very Old Instruction in point of cosmic time—is to forget the misconceptions of the past and press forward to new concepts in the courage of right.

"You are not to be blamed for having doubts, because you live in a world of realities. The man without doubts is the man without love, and the man without love is the man without eternity. There are many kinds of doubt, however.

"As there is no reserve in love, so there is no fear nor

blame. The man who doubts is a good disciple for he keeps the truth alive, and Truth is the beginning and end of all faith and belief in Holy Spirit. The men who will not believe in Holy Spirit are not doubters so much as dissenters from Divinity after they know the facts of eternity. They are the actual 'sinners in Christ'. The way to the truth is by keeping the heart open to the way of the wise men who have found out the path to the light by experience.

"The work of the Lord is now on the increase more than ever before in the history of the race, and we are those who have most to do with it in the years just ahead. You and others will be on the earth-plane and we on the spirit-plane advising. There are many kinds of Love Work to be done in this Vineyard of the Lord, but eventually you will see that men and women are largely the products of their own hates and tempers and yet the worst of them have something within them that is very beautiful and precious. They do not always disclose it but it is there just the same. If you doubt it, you have only to look into their eyes when they are in love with one another and you will be surprised at the understanding you have of their souls . . "

No intelligent man, I submit, could be addressed in such subliminal language night after night and not become possessed of a sense of obligation that he should share it. Miracles long continued cease to be miracles and become commonplaces. But here was instruction, seeming to bear the stamp of authority, that carried beyond anything I had ever heard before, even if the method of receiving it did cease to be necromantic. If it was ironing out many of my own religious complexes, so it should iron out those of others. I gradually began to sense the obligation to pass it along to those who might be interested. It was the natural human reaction—and it altered my whole life's program . . .

STATION-STOP PLANETS

STATION-STOP PLANETS

F YOU are thus learning of these Clairaudient experiences of mine for the first time and are curious to examine the degree of profundities to which the transcriptions attained, you have the previous books, "Thinking Alive" and "Earth Comes", obtainable, to say nothing of that ineffable compilation of New Sermons on the Mount, the so-called "Golden Scripts". ¶ Mary passed from the picture. Half a dozen different women, over two subsequent decades, supplied the feminine polarity requisite for transcription. Spleenish persons who delight in deprecating such phenomena, or rather in deprecating the author of these works, who arise in a shabby sagacity every little while and give it out that they are going to "expose" the true source, or origin, of the intelligence and "tell where it really came from"—usually some mysterious old man or woman who visited me secretly and "slipped" it to me, or from whom I purloined it—clumsily forget that I have the attestments of these various women who worked with me while the wisdom was being recorded in the manner I have narrated. In one case a young man in the Far West suddenly began circulating a similar series of scripts, claiming they had been dictated to him by the same Sages who had by no means intended that I should enjoy a monopoly on their distribution. This overly brilliant young plagiarist forgot that he had no means for checking my original manuscripts, and failed to realize that he was putting out my own editorial correctings and grammatical reconstructions in certain passages. Furthermore, in every case he was infallible at making all the personal deletings I had made—of material too intimate for public circulation. All of which is of no paramount consequence. The point I am making is, a vast compendium of subliminal erudition was being transcribed and accumulated—from sources as mystical to me as they were to my fellows when later I came to publish samples of them—the general effect of which was to "raise my sights" on the whole mammoth enigma of celestiality and creation. Over a million words of it, I repeat. This means that if they were all set in type of this size and the lines placed end to end instead of being printed down a page, they would extend in a single line more than seven miles! It would take in excess of ten minutes, driving in your automobile at forty miles an hour, to transport yourself along this single line of illuminating words. Take out your watch and try to grasp how very long ten minutes may be, traveling continuously past such a stupendous ticker-tape. And what was the "boil-down"? . .

The boil-down was, that the universe was infinitely bigger and grander than anything which man's developing consciousness had visualized to the present. Behind all cosmic creation was the essence of self-motivating and all-pervasive Thought, or Holy Spirit, that men in their littleness proclaimed as God and sought to depict as a likeness to themselves. Celestial Thought "thought fast" and projected electric atoms that built up into the various manifestations of Substances, which in turn built up into all displays of natural phenomena, which in turn built up into exhibits of suns and star-worlds on which human life—or some sort of life—took up residence for purposes of developing the quality and power of its consciousness, or awareness of itself and celestial potentialities. This life was eternal and indestructible as Life, only it manifested in separate and serried forms of biologic organism. The plan and pursuit of the whole celestial scheme was only one plan and pursuit: evolving particles of consciousness to attain to degrees of self-ennoblement where they became gods literally in their own manifestations of exercise and increased the display of the phenomena known as Nature. Men and women, in other words, weren't vile creatures of the dust, or chance accidents of what we call atomic chemistry, but literally "gods in school", serving their educational time either in the classrooms of experience or under the instruction and enlightenment of great Mentors who delayed their own progress up the constellations to give lesser developed beings the benefits of their enhanced intellects and observations about what was taking place in Great Cosmos anyhow. It was all a self-evaluating process, so to speak. Men and women were Gods in School, I say, to emphasize that thought till it truly penetrated their understandings, and as such were required to know all mundane experiencings in order that they might comprehend every phase and aspect of them by conscious participation in their essences. This was the doctrine that gradually unfolded itself. And I sat and partook of it.

SAT and partook of it, I say. And when I had reasonably comprehended—or supposed I had comprehended—the causes for Thought thinking, and for Earth coming, the next proposal concerned the item of how men and women acquired the physical forms that they possessed, making them human creatures, assuming or adopting the forms in which they disclosed themselves in operation on this earth-ball, why and how they had adopted this solar planet as a basis for their operations in the first place and how far they might be going with it, as a proposal in cosmic eugenics and spiritual development. That was the line of logical progression of ideas in the unfolding encyclopedia of facts.

WHAT were men and women? They were cosmic bits of God, to put it in ecclesiastical terms, who had found this solar planet off here in this particular "northern" corner of the heavenly galaxies, on which to perform unto themselves over untold aeons and develop their consciousness into pattern that did justice to the plan of creation activating the whole celestial display. That, in a nutshell, was the whole of it. But where had they come from originally? Had they derived biologically from the essences of this residence-planet, as the purblind scientist assumed? No, they had not, according to this New Intelligence now being revealed by personages who called themselves The Masters. There WERE biologic forms that DID derive from the major essences of this particular planet, cosmically considered. They were indigenous forms. But were humankind, strictly speaking, of these? I was to have the intelligence gradually conveyed to me that they were not. Men and women, in the creative sense, seemed to have been derived from some other planet, or some other set of star worlds, from which they had voyaged celestially to arrive on earth and find it habitable.

Odd as the thought may seem, it bore aspects of rationality when I came to consider some of the phenomena permeating society in respect to their primeval origins. Looking back over twenty years of the Master instruction—or enlightenment—I find the generalized picture in my intellect of a growth or development of indigenous earth-forms in the biologic sense gradually creeping up to, and perfecting, the ape. All that had gone before this point seemed to be pretty much in line with what the evolutionary scientists contended. But somewhere along in the grand procession of evolution, just after the cat and ape had attained to maximum physical facility, SOMETHING HAD HAPPENED!

That "something" as I came to be instructed upon it, seemed to be, that a vast horde of migrating spirits from a wholly separate distinction of creation, arrived within the aura of this physically habitable earth and began to manifest in the forms and creations they found here. Maybe it was all phantasmagoria. Maybe it did happen. The thing in which I found myself interested was how

the proposition fitted into what we have come to discover about humankind in its earliest stages of mundane residence. Could it have happened? . . that was the thing. WHY it should require to become a happening was something else, and in a different category of celestial eugenics. I took the arriving intelligence in its stride and sought to make of it what I could . . or rather, what I would.
I found it could be electrifying.
Men and women ARE different creatures than anything else observable in the form of created life on this solar planet. The evolutionist says that this is due to the fact of gradual improvement upon lower forms. But the evolutionist doesn't go overly much out of his way to explain why and wherein there are forms similar to man that haven't evolved, or developed, from the early forms. To be specific, we have the great apes with us in the jungles of tropical countries today equally as primordial as when "human evolution" is said to have begun. Terrestrial conditions over the whole planet have not been so unique as to "evolve" one section of the ape-family and pass by another section. Yet the biologist, lacking the secret of the unknown human ingredient, solemnly asks us to accept that it happened.
The Subliminal Mentors, at whose knees I was sitting nightly over a period of years and who declared that it was happening—my sudden instruction—because I had made some sort of prenatal pact that it should happen

when I had arrived at an effective stage of my career to make it generally public, the Subliminal Mentors contended that it didn't happen. How they came by their knowledge of what did happen, I had no means of knowing and still have no means, and I publish their assertions for what they seem to be worth. But their general explanation for the events that had gone on, making human society what we find it in history and what we observe it to be today, embodied the hypothesis that "people from somewhere" came to this earth in discarnate aspects, found animal forms here convenient to their use and to their cosmic self-betterment, and proceeded to appropriate and inhabit those forms in their own rights, drawing what benefits from such residence as they could. I submit you the whole of it for what it seems to be worth. Admittedly it does explain a lot that to the present has been abstruse.

These "star guests"—for we have every right to term them that—found conditions here on this terrestrial ball precisely congenial for the development of their consciousness by the expedients of experience in fleshly forms, and settled down upon this planet to remain. And by all the signs they have remained, up to this hour in terrestrial history.

They came here and settled down here to "get something" by residing in the indigenous beast forms which they found here and when they had achieved it we had the beginnings of HUMAN evolution as distinct from primate evolution. The bodies were in a measure the same, but the spiritual essence inhabiting those physical organisms was different. And so the human essences have gone on breeding and multiplying organically and the animal forms that were not interrupted by the intrusion of the star guests, have also gone on breeding and multiplying, and today we have the exhibit of the two in propinquity—the primate inside the cage at the zoo, and his "visiting guest" outside, paying admission to view him, but the "visiting guest" enwrapped in a physical ensemble which he has improved or "evolved" because of his surpassing psychical difference.

We have two orders of animate spirit, in other words, when considering the human as compared to the simian. In the human there is the Higher Essence that came here a-visiting and remained here to sublimate the indigenous primate organism into the half-monkey and half-angel that we call the human race today. In the ape pattern we have the indigenous pattern of biologic consciousness still going its hectic way to what "improvement" it can develop with the star-guest mortal in supervising competition with it.

It is something to think about.

Today we have human beings procreating human beings from these sublimated monkey-organisms, just so long as the parents are human. And we have the ape-forms always and forever procreating apes just so long as the parents are primate. Something distinctive transfers in every case of conception as between each form so that they never mix up. What is it?

We as human beings—we might as well face it—are "angels in the forms of apes" and we keep on breeding our progeny as little angels in the forms of little apes. But the ape goes on breeding apes to the seventieth generation. Darwin and his fellow biologists sought to establish a "missing link" between the two forms, and from time to time various evolutionary scientists all over the world have raucously proclaimed that by turning up a bit of bone in China or Java they have discovered the connection. But what they seem to have discovered is merely the physical attachment between the primate and the star-guest, as the latter brought the primate up toward the organically sublimated.

And marvel though we will, that hypothesis makes sense ✯

F COURSE, considered practically in the payment of today's grocery bill, or meeting the problems of socialism and communism, or trying to decide whether Keith's has a better movie tonight than the local Bijou, the origins of our species are of academic interest only. What difference does it make to us as individuals whether we descended from star-guests or antediluvian Chinamen? But in our practical problems of incarnation and reincarnation, the lore is of stupendous

interest to us. We are "angel-apes" trying to get out of the inhibitions of the animalistic and climb upward and onward to our waiting celestiality, but the experience nonetheless does hold profit for us.

We are, apparently, Star Guests on this planet who find ourselves encased in bodies of primates in order to learn something spiritually ennobling. That we have been here for aeons and will undoubtedly be here for aeons longer, atom bombs and H-bombs to the contrary notwithstanding, is nothing in point of cosmic time. What is Time in eternity? The real issue is, by giving a tuppence of credit to the theory, we have a stupendous lot made clear to us that only yesterday was black enigma. At least we are lifted out of the category of beings made conscious by chemical affinities. We are lifted from the category of beings who perish as the animal perishes, that is, physically. We live over and over and over, apparently, in successive ape-sublimates, and gradually pass off to ineffable states of spirit, in extenuation of the consciousness apparently begun in some solar system outside our computing.

It is all part of the growth we get for godhood.

Our spirits are eternal and non-perishable! . . that is the basic tenet underlying all the instruction from this source that I have ever received or transcribed. Once get that in our minds and all creation and mortality takes on an altered aspect.

We are residents of all Cosmos, apparently. We dwell

at present upon this planet Earth. What planet we may have come from originally is immaterial, since its location can only be marked by the position of all the other planets, hanging in a void, and outside of which there is no means of determining location.

The thing that I learned—or was instructed in—leaving me somewhat breathless when I had come to grasp it, was, that certain Earth Forms were evolving upward upon this earth-planet, indigenous to this particular terrestrial ball as the evolutionary scientists proclaim. But what the evolutionary scientists do not know is, that somewhere back in the Eocene or Oligocene periods, fifty to thirty million years ago, there came a great migration of alien spirits to this planet from some other world in interstellar space, who settled down here and began to cohabit with the animal forms it discovered developing here, producing a hybrid race of beings, half-celestial and half-bestial that gave us the unspeakable Sodomic period described in the Bible.

The trouble with the Bible is, that the time-element recorded is all wrong. The ancient authors of the Bible, having some psychic inkling of what happened but supposing that this Earth-Planet was the center of the universe, tried to fit the events attending upon the Great Migration into the time-calendar of the past four thousand years. Actually, the time consumed or covered was millions of years. The ancient Hebrews were trying to apply these celestial occurrences to the history of their particular race, and they took liberties with Time, striving to compress it down into reasonably acceptable terms of the last few thousand years.

These superior beings from another celestial planet, cohabiting with the earth-forms of life they discovered here on their arrival, began to fill up the earth with a race of monsters that were neither bestial, human, nor divine. The result was a confusion that almost defeated the original plans of creation. Beast forms and celestial forms were fused together in an insufferable bastard creation from which certain specimens of the two creations are evincing even down here in the twentieth century.

It was this Great Abominatory Period, apparently, that produced the notion of "redemption" with which the Bible is very full. The celestial race had to be "saved" from its admixture of species with earth-beasts. And curiously enough, therein lay the reason for the arrival of the Christ Avatar upon this planet . . which will presently be expounded. He had to "head up" the job of separating the two forms of creation—the people of the Original Migration and the Earth Beasts with whom they cohabited—and get them back to their original status. And this is the work of "redemption" that is the true explanation for all the processes of "salvation" that maintained even down into modern times.

N THE SIXTH chapter of Genesis we find these words: "And it came to pass, when men began to multiply upon the face of the earth, and daughters were born unto them, that the Sons of God saw the daughters of men that they were fair; and they took of them wives of all which they chose.

And the Lord said, My spirit shall not always strive with man, for that he is also flesh: yet his days shall be an hundred and twenty years.

And there were giants in the earth in those days; and also after that, when the Sons of God came in unto the daughters of men, and they bear children to them, the same became mighty men which were of old, men of renown. And God saw that the wickedness of man was great in the earth and that every imagination of the thoughts of his heart was only evil continually.

And it repented the Lord that He had made man upon the earth and it grieved him at His heart. And the Lord said, I will destroy man whom I have created, from the face of the earth; both man and beast, and the creeping thing, and the fowls of the air; for it repenteth Me that I have made them.

So much for Holy Writ.
According to the ancient legend, the earth was subsequently introduced to the catastrophe of the Deluge. We are told of the holiness of Noah and how he was

instructed to prepare the ark and save himself and family and two of every living species. All of it seems to have been an elemental and somewhat inaccurate way of recording a great cosmic truth. The human race was saved through Noah, the Flood subsided, his progeny multiplied and became "all of one speech"—which produced next the Tower of Babel episode and the confounding of tongues. The human race was prone to get into trouble again if it talked the same international language, so the Lord must "take steps" . .

The Lord was busy taking a whole lot of steps, it appears, in those ancient days, considering the cussedness of the race He had created.

Anyhow, universal speech had the quietus put on it and people began to jabber as it pleased them by localities. The ancient chroniclers were anxious to get to Abram and explain how the whole works were handed over to the Hebrews. They did get to Abram, and he was bidden to get himself up out of the land of Egypt and have all the kingdoms of the world presented to him. So we have the tale of the fuss wth Lot about pasturage for flocks in and around Bethel, and Lot moving westward toward Sodom and Gomorrah—where an unprecedented thunderstorm was presently to occur and make life exceeding difficult. In the 13th verse of the 13th chapter of Genesis, we therefore get down to the fiery destruction of Sodom and Gomorrah.

All of which was a beautiful mix-up of cosmic event,

catching the essentials of what happened but not the correct motives nor chronology.

Men of that ancient time were striving, of course, to get the whole piebald mystery of creation into a few hundred years and words and create a logical background for the claim that the Hebrews were inheritors of whatever could be found on earth that wasn't nailed down. Hence the badly mixed-up version presented us in Holy Writ.

Why haven't the Biblical scholars paid more attention to this significant assertion: "The Sons of God saw the daughters of men that they were fair; and they took of them wives of all which they chose"?

The Sons of God? What Sons of God, and where had they come from? Genesis makes no particular explanation for the creation of any Sons of God as contradistinguished from the descendants of Adam. And these mysterious "daughters of men"—where did they originate, especially in view of the fact that Adam and Eve had no female progeny? For that matter, how came it that there were females over in the Land of Nod when Cain got romantic and decided he needed conjugal affection? Who created these people in the Land of Nod? Where was Nod in respect to the Garden of Eden? If the Bible be the infallible "word of God," as the fundamentalists insist that we accept, why weren't explanations of record about those Nod folks? Was there a contemporaneous creation over in the Land of Nod, and if so, why has Genesis remained silent about it? Why wouldn't one creation be just as consequential as the other? Let's face these discrepancies. We can't have the Bible both accurate and inaccurate—it has to be one or the other.

The New Doctrine that seemed to be arriving for me over the Clairaudient Route had it that "the daughters of men" was a refined way of describing the bestial female earth-forms that were coming to evolutionary development on this puzzling earth-planet. The "Sons of God" were the people of the arriving migration, coming, or finding, this solar satellite here in universal space, twirling about our sixth-rate sun, and settling down to seduce these female indigenous people and give them child that were neither one nor the other—neither beasts indigenous to this earth nor celestial spirits coming from another system of creation.

According as I have interpreted the celestial scripts I have received upon the subject, we might crassly put it that the "daughters of earth" were nothing more nor less than female apes of a sort, although we do have references made constantly to the fact that the arriving "Sons of God" by no means incarnated in the similar ape-forms directly. They tried out incarnation in certain biologic cat-forms first, as we shall have described for us in the succeeding Master Message.

The point, from this twentieth-century angle of observation, is not important. What concerns us most vitally is, that there WERE indigenous earth-forms as females to be seduced, and "Sons of God" to seduce them. The progeny seems to have been antediluvian man, or better, prehistoric man—half brute and half divine spirit. These, presented with mortal bodies that had all the physical attributes of the apes and all the spiritual attributes of the "Sons of God from another planet" gave us the human race that must be "redeemed" from the heritage of its edenic lust.

Here then, is your famous "missing link" for which the evolutionary scientists search so hopelessly.

THE MARSUPIALS may indeed have descended from trees and begun to perfect a superior order of beastly creation, somewhere back in Eocene or Oligocene times. But that a superior order of interstellar spirits began arriving within our earth's conditions from some distant center of creation—where the life was much further advanced—is outside the domain of the biologic scientist. He has no way of proving it and little to call it to his attention, excepting as the folklore of all ancient peoples seems to have some mystical reference to a Sodomic period when "men cohabited with beasts." When we explore the higher akashic records, however, from which the Masters are apparently getting their information, we come upon the explanation, weird as it seems, that the "mixture of the breeds" must have happened. And the earth had to be "purged by flood and fire" to get rid of the monsters and "abominations" that had resulted.

In confirmation of all this, on the 4th of March, 1929, in Altadena, California, without the slightest solicitation on my part, I suddenly began "taking down" the following psychic transcription concerning this most significant of happenings.

I reprint it for you for what it is worth.

Before you get into its official attestment, however, it might not be out of place to call some reliable geologic facts to your attention.

There have been, according to the biologic scientists, something like 27 "eras" or "periods" of life on this planet and it should by no means come amiss to have them tabulated for us in this volume, that we may have them available for reference when reading volumes of this series which are still to come. Supposing we look them over—

EARTH'S BYGONE ERAS

1. ARCHEOZOIC Era—(Oldest known life)— 2,000 million years ago;
2. PROTEROZOIC Era—(Primitive marine life)— 1,100 million years ago;
3. CAMBRIAN Period—(Trilobites)—800 million to 700 million years ago; (Paleozoic Era begins)
4. ORDOVICIAN Period—(Fresh water fishes)— 400 million years ago;

5. SILURIAN Period—(Air-breathing animals)—350 million years ago;
6. DEVONIAN Period—(Insects)—300 million years ago;
7. CARBONIFEROUS Period—(Reptiles)—250 million years ago;
8. PERMIAN Period—(Mollusks)—200 million years ago (End of Paleozoic Era)
9. TRIASSIC Period—(Beginning of Mammals)—175 million years ago (Mesozoic Era begins)
10. JURASSIC Period—(Development of Bird Life)—150 million years ago;
11. CRETACEOUS Period—(Placental mammals)—100 million years ago (End of Mesozoic Era)
12. EOCENE Period—(Two-legged erect animals)—50 million years ago (Cenazoic Era starts)
13. OLIGOCENE Period—(Great Apes appeared)—30 million years ago;
14. MIOCENE Period—(Heidelberg Man; probably the time of the Migration)—17 million years ago;
15. PLIOCENE Period—(Cro-Magnon man; the Edenic period)—10 million years ago;
16. PLEISTOCENE Period—(Fire and Flood period)—500,000 years ago;
17. ARYAN Era—(Spiritual perceivings)—10,000 years ago;
18. CHINESE Era—(through Confucius, 500 B. C.)—4,254 years ago;

19. BABYLON-SUMARIAN Era—(Euphrates civilization)—4,048 years ago;
20. EGYPTIAN Era—(Rise of Ikhnaton's concepts) 3,388 years ago;
21. CRETAN Era—(Modern civilization on Crete)— 3,000 years ago;
22. HEBRAIC Era—(Pre-Bible times)—2,500 years ago;
23. GREEK Era—(Rise of Hellenic States)—2,400 years ago;
24. ROMAN Era—(Times of Christ)—2,100 to 1700 years ago;
25. ISLAMIC Era—(Rise of Mohammadism)—1,316 years ago;
26. GALLIC-ITALIAN Era—(Renaissance period)— 750 years ago;
27. BRITISH-AMERICAN Era—(Current times)— 500 years ago to present.

The human race in its present pattern, we can see from the foregoing, has been upon this planet anywhere between 17 million and 10 million years, and will probably dwell upon it 10 to 17 million years more—if the celestial salvation of the species seems to require that long, atom and H-bombs to the contrary notwithstanding. The Great Avatar—assuming we have made contact with Him, as we have reason for believing—has some pertinent remarks to make about universal detruction by atom bombs, take note, to which we shall give ear at the proper place. The great plan of salvation, however, goes forward regardless of Time in the cosmic calculations. There is a massive job to be done and it is being done—and our interests are entirely concerned with understanding it and assisting as we can. Such being our pure intent, suppose we give ear to the words of the Great Avatar Himself, while He explains for our inhibited understanding exactly what took place on this earth-ball millions of years in the past, making His services necessary . . .

The Great Abomination

MY DEARLY BELOVED:
There are questions of truth troubling you. I say, be of calm confidence. I am He who was equally tried, and found peace and consideration of My Father, even as ye do find it when you consider Me.

Harken while I tell you of truths that convince you I am speaking to you indeed. There are mysteries that ye know not of. I speak of them tonight.

Mankind was not always as ye see him walking the earth at present; mankind was possessed of physical features making him hideous unto God. Mankind had queer members, too potent of evil to be long tolerated. Mankind had features of the Beast. He was of eagle-head and lion body. Great was his brutishness.

From the evil which he did when he had come to earth and found earth-forms upon it, was he cleansed by fire and flood. He came through vast ordeals which shaped his physiognomy as ye do see it now. He had strange claws and stranger tissues. He was of the Brute and yet not of it. From the depths of degradation to which he had sunk he arose with skull of ape; he walked upright on two legs; he became the prey of beasts instead of hunter. He made for himself habitations in trees and prowled by night seeking food.

Deep, deep, was his ignorance. Little more than beast was he indeed, with almost no spark of divinity left to him ⚐

The Father was touched by creation gone wrong. The principle of Thought Incarnate made carnate had sported, as it were and man had resulted, not as ye know him now but half-bird and half-lion man, that did make abominations unto himself.

Millions upon millions of years ago was man thus, and he came from races of angels mixed with beasts. Slow hath been his separation since. Out of the abomination he hath separated, angel and brute, and goeth back the way he came. The brute dieth in one direction, the angel ascendeth in another. Understand ye this?

Man hath a mission upon this planet. He was to be its keeper for a purpose. He was to know it for a dwelling of spirits who had lessons in flesh to be taught them. They were not to know where they were. They were to depart from the Godhead periodically to learn of existence apart from Divinity. They were to know pain and suffering and sorrow to make them fit subjects for higher planes. That was the first intent and meaning of earth as earth.

Hear ye My words, that ye may be wise in the generation wherein ye do dwell among men, that ye may instruct them in their destinies in flesh.

LIFE came to earth from the planets of the star-sun Sirius—so called by men. On those planets centereth Thought Incarnate, ruling that which ye know as the universe. Life came to the solar planet Earth at the behest of Thought Incarnate presiding over all planet-systems and watching the movements thereof. Man was despatched to this small planet Earth as a prison of pain for education. Came he first as Thought himself, made manifest in physical flesh over many generations. Gradually did he learn lessons and wax vigorous of stamina and deceit. Gradually did he take unto himself knowledge of heavenly origin, making manifest his abominations in experiment with thought-forms. Over many aeons did he wax stronger and stronger, priding himself on his infallibility of structure and endurance. His heart was heavenly in divine creation, his body was physically handicapped by weight. Slowly he acquired proficiency in altering his body.

Head was first bird-like, as I have disclosed to you. His hands were like claws, conceived for destruction. Feet were reversible, making him locomote forwards or backwards. Conception was twofold: by physical contact yet lacking organs of generation externally. Also he did create by thought, clothing his thought in etheric covering and calling it Material. Contact creation was made cell by cell, male and female embracing and leaving on the ground excretions which when developed became new life. Understand ye this? . .

Man did come to know pain of education, but having come, he practiced abominations as relief from tedium. Now mark well Mine instruction—

Man had head like eagle and body like lion. Not as present earthly man was he in any form. Spirit of angel had he in his heart, but not for long. Man had opportunity to put Thought into practice, to create abominations because he had no means of expression otherwise. To create Thought Forms and abominations gave him relief from tedium upon a planet where all his physical wants were supplied without effort.

Know ye that he had no body when first he came to earth; he looked upon beast and bird and chose body most likely to give him attributes producing qualities of spirit. Now mark you—

THE SPIRIT of man was essentially Thought Incarnate, coming to earth and taking body of beast for self-expression on the physical plane. Thereat came tedium. Thereat came desire for relief from that tedium. Thereat did he make mock of Thought Celestial and abominations grew up on every hand. Beast was progenitor of angelic spirit; angelic spirit was progenitor of beast. Strange beyond belief was the bastardy thereof 🙰

Man lost his lion shape; he walked as ape. He lost his bird cranium having beak and crossed eyes. He came into possession of hand having thumb. He made use of tool. Slowly did he lose control over thought-generation. More and more sank he into sporting with etheric forms of matter. Matter became his fetish and his shibboleth. Matter became his world.

Spirit Divine did he start from; spirit materialistic did he acquire until all interest in spirit, as spirit, departed. Now come I to Thought Incarnate permitting such abominations to occur . .

Know ye that life is ever self-perpetuating; it cannot die to extinction. Matter changeth form but likewise it cannot die to extinction. Is this not confirmed by your science of the present? Matter endureth and is essentially constant. Only form altereth.

Life and Matter are forms of union of particles that have Thought in manifestation behind them and in them. Life is eternal as life. It cannot proceed from many causes but only itself can bring about its extinction. Life is not a physical manifestation excepting as present-day man conceives. It is a form of union with forces of Thought Incarnate made by principles of ether. It cometh and goeth in different manifestations to the senses, but so long as Thought thinketh and so long as ether endureth, so long hath life its existence, which is forever! . .

Know ye therefore that the forms of spirits having come to earth from the Sirian planets could never be destroyed as spirits. They could be changed in physical manifestation but only they themselves could cease to exist. So therefore no decree of Thought Incarnate—who for purposes of worldly utility ye call the Father—could banish them from the state that is known as existence. Causes of malformation of created order, shapes delirious, they might be. Shapes hideous to think upon they might make in diabolical caprice and dwell therein, but they must ever live their lives with knowledge of good and evil and pain and suffering.

Dumb beast orders were forms of creation experimented with by Thought Incarnate as a means for making spirit to know Itself. They were made especially and separately that spirit might learn different lessons from each. But man gone creative, as it were, transformed beast into strange anomalies.

SO VAST had been the wickedness of bastardy that forms were fusing together into monsters having no purpose but self-destruction. So vast had become the practice of abomination that even male and female were becoming indistinguishable. So great was the practice of that crime called Sodomy that men and animals were growing interchangeable of spirit and structure. Man was beastly and beast was manlike. Spirit knew not itself, whether it were divine or whether it were experiment of Thought Incarnate.

They had so interchanged that they could no longer be accepted by the Host on Sirian planets as divine.

Spirit released at physical death was not of pure aspiration toward the Father but rather a downward trend toward darkness and brutishness. The Mark of the Beast lingered even unto spiritual freedom at perishment of physical form. Always the freed spirit sought wickedness of manifestation. Always it longed to return to beast to gratify physical expression in abominations. Aeon unto aeon it worked, not back toward the Godhead but toward the Pit of Destruction.

The Godhead was incensed and dismayed. Creation had gone astray. Man had become as Thought Incarnate, knowing good and yet doing evil.

Whereupon came necessity for the cleansing of ALL physical forms. Pure beast must be preserved as beast; pure angel-man must be preserved as angel-man. Thus was a vast catastrophe decided upon. Ice from polar seas was to be melted by passing sun and released upon continents of monsters.

Great was the destruction thereof. Man was appalled by the ending of the cycle of creation in its own right. Forms perished to stay perished. No longer could life make physical vehicles by thought. Forms existing in purity were preserved. Bastards, monsters, and anomalies were destroyed. No longer could they propagate. Pure species were saved and pronounced sterile unto all but themselves.

This sterility could not have been decreed on monsters because man had so taken unto himself powers of creation by Thought that sex sterility or lack of it would not have mattered. He could have created without recourse to organs.

Now be advised, when came the Great Catastrophe those who perished physically were not dead spiritually but they sloughed off their monstrous features and were known en masse for spirits again but without physical equipment ☨

KNOW THAT HERE ENTERED I, THE SON OF THOUGHT INCARNATE! . .

CAME I to this planet at the Father's behest. Man was pure ape or pure spirit. He had escaped the Great Catastrophe in areas where his species was clean. He was beastly but cleanly beastly and he knew not the scheme of creating by Thought that which pleased his whim ☨

Came I first to earth on a mission. The Father desired that knowledge of good and evil be restrained. Man was to suffer and die as beast, returning to the planets of the star-sun Sirius on physical death of beastly body. But came I to the Father with better plan.

The world of men could be cleansed of the beast by my instruction. Over countless generations could man be lifted back slowly to his lost angelic status. Life upon life he could live and perish, and live again. Slowly he could come up through new forms of ape-man until he was indeed a god restored to the Godhead! Not through varied forms but through manifestations of the same form, could he regain unto ennoblement. And the same form meant the ape-form.

Thus was Reincarnation born as men of earth understand Reincarnation today. So man came to remain in possession of ape-body. Man had used the ape-form for thousands of generations, finding it more efficient for his caprice than lion-form. Thus was he manifesting when catastrophe overtook all creation.

Therefore know ye, that ape-forms are pure forms of species but man hath appropriated ape-forms and improved upon them until ye do be angel apes yourselves writing thus in your domiciles tonight.

Man as spirit hath no form that is constant. Man as spirit hath any form which serveth constructive purpose in making Love externalize. But man on the physical plane maintaineth the Ape Form of the Great Catastrophe ✣

My dear ones, I have instructed you with some degree and depth of understanding. The time is ripe for such enlightenment for you. More have I to reveal, but I go for a time. Tomorrow night we resume . . .

WHAT a lot was explained if I could credit the profundities of this message! Nowhere in sacred or profane literature had I ever found its equal. Vaguely, of course, I was able to discern behind it all the same chronology of events recorded in the Biblical Genesis. But how altered in significance! Apparently the authors of of the Book of Genesis—whoever they had been—had received an inkling of the facts from ancient times and simplified the story into an epitome of the history of the original Chosen People, making it brief and plausible to satisfy the understanding of a primitive people. I could comprehend that, and make due allowances. But the thing appalling me was obtaining information that rationalized Reincarnation.

Based on the explanation given me in this message, Reincarnation made the profoundest sense. Men and women were working out a great cosmic redemption and the "Christ People" so-called were uniformly their mentors, inspiring them back to their lost spiritual heritage. Christ Himself had a meaning, when viewed in the light of it that no orthodox theology offered me. But what I particularly desired to have told me was the origin of the Being whom the Great Teacher described as "the Father" . .

That was to come later, I was to find. I had many more messages to take before I was ready for it . .

But no enlightenment was withheld.

SALVATION MAKES SENSE

SALVATION MAKES SENSE

YOU can credit it or deprecate it, but when this sort of instruction began coming to me over the Clairaudient route, I felt no little consternation. Never, I say, had I encountered anything like it in my experience. My concept of the growth and development of human life was the popular biologic concept, that man's physical organism was the finished product of millions of years of "natural selection" and adaptation to environment following the earth's geologic changes. It was an easy and simple explanation for man being the half bestial and half intellectual creature which modern society beholds him—in fact, too easy and too simple. Natural selection or adaptation to environment didn't account for the curious circumstance that men and apes from days immemorial have gone on living and breeding in identical environments and yet men have stayed men and apes have stayed apes. Saying that they had a "common ancestor" was one way of rationalizing a biologic headache, but it didn't account at all for the demonstrated fact that the two strains went on breeding true to one another, millennia by millennia, no "evolution" being apparent in the last half-dozen million years. You can train an ape today to wear a plug hat, ride a bicycle, smoke a cigar, and sort picture blocks, but he will still remain an ape unto the twelfth generation. Man in some of his remote habitats may have less intelligence than the bread-and-butter run of ordinary circus chimpanzees, but he will still go on breeding true human beings insofar as we can discover or observe. Of course the sequences of our observation are far too brief for us to determine definitely whether much evolution is going on in this, our current millennium, but certainly man is making little progress biologically as the generations succeed each other within our scope of knowledge. If anything, man physically today seems definitely retrograding as he loses his physical faculties by reason of residence in great cities where Nature makes little demands on him for animal survival. The subject is moot, however, and can't be argued pro or con effectively within the scope of this work. I had all of the perplexities of the biologist confronting me, I say, in March of 1929 when I began this altered type of intelligence out of what seemed to me "the higher reaches of Time and Space." The challenge I faced was whether or not the clairaudient "enlightenment" made any better sense than the rationalizings of the Darwinians.

Of course, the dogmatic statements made in one paper on the subject of man's mystical past weren't sufficient of themselves to prove anything conclusively. Hundreds of pages more had to be transcribed and studied before the new suggestions "sugared off" into anything like convictions. But queerly enough, my chief aid in that quarter seemed to come from observations of what I might call very ancient religious practices and symbolisms, that man in his present-day erudition—or lack of it—assumed to be merely the spiritual vagaries of a childlike imaginative orthodoxy. For instance, the sphinxes and Bird and Animal gods of peoples like the early Egyptians.

A sphinx, as the commonest schoolchild is aware, is a representation of a half-human, half-animal creature, with the head of a human being and body of a lion. Why should ancient peoples, wise enough and cultured enough to erect such astounding structures as the Great Pyramid or the Temple at Karnac, dabble around in such monumental fantasies as sculpturing human heads on feline bodies? What could such an anomaly possibly represent and how had they conceived of it originally? Were they trying to depict their ancient deities or potentates as being intellectual after the human pattern but physically agile and dexterous after the feline pattern? Or were those ancient peoples the more sagaciously aware of deeper mystical origins of the distinctive human race and caused these apparent monstrosities to be wrought in commemoration of something that we, in our cosmic illiteracy, consider only fantasy and vivid religious imagination?

For instance, I asked myself, could it be true and logical that these long-ago "pagan" peoples knew about the original migration of the Star Guests to this solar planet and the crossing of breeds with the creatures of earth? Did they know of the issue of half-god, half-animal progeny typified by a creature with the god's cranium and face, and the earthly animal's body—in the case of the sphinx, the cat?

Were sphinxes the most ancient of monuments to the Great Sodomic Period, when these star-guest spirits were emerging in organic patterns from the feline into the ape-forms?

Today, beholding the ruins of them, the most illiterate of human beings accepts capriciously that having no other gods to worship and admiring the lion for his prowess, the ancient Mediterraneans merely clapped a human head on a lion's body and cried childishly: "See what we made!" expecting it should be worshiped because of the union of mental and physical virtues that it depicted. The human mind has been productive of greater absurdities.

Perhaps, on the other hand, the sphinx was no more meant as an object of worship than the statue to General Sherman at the entrance to Central Park is meant as an object of worship for Americans of today. Just as Sherman's monument commemorates sterling leadership of the Northern forces in the war between the States, so the sphinx monument might commemorate mystical transition of the "angel-spirit" out of its original feline organism, a war of a sort between the spiritual and physical in the peculiar predicament the Star-Guests invited by having progeny with lower forms of life indigenous to the earth. It was something to muse upon and conjecture as one would.

Then there were those "hawk-headed" gods of the ancient Egyptians—why put heads of birds on human shoulders, either? Was it only another aspect of the same pre-Sodomic period of which my message spoke? It was something to think about, I say. Also that information about the planets of the star-sun Sirius, that is commonly known to us as the Dog Star. Could it be possible that Sirius had anything resembling planets turning about it that could be any seat of "Thought Incarnate"?

Well, I was "in" for some perturbing surprises . .

IRIUS, by far the brightest fixed star in the sky, is easily found in Canis Major, a little below Orion, and was mythologically regarded as one of the hounds held in leash by Orion, Procyon in Canis Minor being the other. A line drawn from the Pleiades through the three stars of Orion's belt will pass it closely; straight lines connecting it with Procyon and Betelguese will constitute a nearly equilateral triangle. Aldebaran, Betelguese, Sirius and Rigel, all star-suns of the first magnitude, form a lozenge-shaped figure with Orion's belt in the center.

Ptolemy, in the second century, ranked Sirius among the red stars. Now it appears to be white and is an extremely brilliant object, its light being 324 times as great as any stars of the sixth magnitude. It is about 1,000,000 times as far from us as the sun, and its mass is about twenty times as big. Viewed by the spectroscope, its chief lines are those of incandescent hydrogen with feebler lines of sodium and magnesium. The mercuric content is also said to be heavy. But now get the following—

Some irregular movements of Sirius led to the belief that some heavenly body existed near enough to it to produce a perturbation, and a son of Alvin Clark, of Boston, Mass., on January 31, 1862, discovered what appeared to be a mammoth planet revolving about Sirius as its sun, completing its stupendous orbit in something like 49 of our solar years. None of this was of my knowledge at the time I took the March 1929 message. I discovered it all afterwards when I started reading up on the Dog Star.

I found that the spectroscope further showed it to be approaching our solar system at the rate of 336 miles per minute. If it were coming straight toward us, it might eventually overtake and crash into us. Sirius has, however, a cross-component of motion which in time will take it far distant into parts of the heavens which we might almost describe as uncharted. Where is it going, and why? But even if this "Seat of the Godhead" were aiming directly for our sun at the rate of 336 miles per minute, it would take such an enormous time for its arrival that its brightness would not increase ten percent in 10,000 years.

The question as to whether Sirius is attended by a satellite or accompanied by a companion sun, seems still to be disputed. But it has been established since 1862 that there is a definite center of gravity around which the pair of heavenly bodies seems to revolve at distances of 1,800 millon miles in a period of 48 or 49 years. The important thing that impressed me in the whole of it was: Sirius for uncounted millions of years has been coming TOWARD us, and is still coming toward us. How significant is that, cosmically speaking, that we are hourly and momentarily drawing nearer and nearer to the Godhead, or the Godhead—give it any definition you will—is drawing nearer and nearer toward us? At least it seems better than going away from it!

Then, while I was meditating upon this business of "angel-spirits" migrating to this sixth-rate little solar ball, on the 5th of March, 1929 came another dissertation on the subject that gave food for still more thought.
¶ I shall come back many times to digressions on Astronomy before the end of this present book is reached, but for the present consider what the "Master" had to say upon the topic of "The Rage of Felines" . .

Again I submit it to you for what you may consider it worth 🙢 🙢

The Rage of Felines

MY DEARLY BELOVED:

I AM come to you in that I want you to know that I am He who instructeth you for reasons of loving consideration for your identities. I am He who was sent unto Man, even as ye have been sent unto Man, for a purpose. I am He who was instrumental in saving men from extinction as men, and causing them to return unto the Father in ways of thought.

Know ye that thousands upon thousands of years ago came two vast catastrophes. One was the flooding of all abominate parts of the earth; the other was the fiery destruction of life in countries that were not affected by that flood.

The species that had thus survived that deluge were purified by fire, for fire could destroy individual monsters where flood destroyed wholesale. By flood and by fire were monsters destroyed and man left clean in ape form, which he hath since pursued.

Know that I did make representations unto the Heavenly Host that I would come to earth and aid man to regain his lost angelic status over tremendous periods of time. Know that I offered my life as mortal, not once but many times. Know that in form on form I have come and gone in Matter since the days of the Great Purification. Ever as Spirit Made Manifest for purposes of divine instruction have I come and gone in races of the ape men .. Know that I have been constant and continual redeemer of the ape race. Know that ye have been my devoted disciples, accompanying Me or interpreting Me times beyond count.

Races have come and nations have arisen to mighty prominence; races have gone and nations have sunk beneath the desert sands since first we did manifest in Matter for the self-degraded ape men. See ye thus how the Plan came about ..

EN were practitioners of whoredoms; they were consorts of beasts; they had filled the earth with abominations, being neither man nor beast, even as your Scriptures have informed you, but informed you wrongly concerning the time and the place.

The cleansing time came. The species were made sterile unto all but themselves. Knowledge of Thought-Creation was taken from man—WHICH IS WHAT IS MEANT BY MEN AND WOMEN COMING TO KNOW THEIR OWN NAKEDNESS.

Man knew not his own nakedness when he was beast himself. Came I to earth to drive him from his innocence of concept making mischiefs against world-species. Came I to earth to make him master of himself. Came I to earth to make man to realize the divinity within himself until it controlled and put down the beast. Now harken . .

The beast which man had raised was not as other beasts made by Thought Incarnate for growth of spirit-particles in their own awareness. The beast which man had made, and dwelt in, was made of evil. It made the other beasts fearful, and being ill with fear they defended themselves as their group-spirits prompted, that they might survive.

See ye now how certain animals came to possess ferocious natures? Those which were most like unto man in his earliest forms were perplexed and frightened by his Thought-Abominations. They cared not for man's creations as their mates. They turned from such monstrosities in fright, and their terror hath marked their generations born since.

Have ye no cognizance of the ferocity of species aligned to man's earliest forms? Judge ye then the natures of such ferocities and how they came to be what ye perceive them.

THE FELINES WERE MOST SAVAGE BECAUSE MOST OUTRAGED, and greatest was their alarm at reproduction. So did they hate man most and become his fiercest enemies.

Let Me explain something else—

Man as man was never brutish by divine intent. Man

was created angel in potential power and privilege. His sojourn on this solar planet was meant in the Beginning to be brief. He was to know Ordeal and Pain and Endurance, that he might return to the Host wise beyond them because of his experience.

Know that he did bring with him to earth certain propensities of spirit toward Godlike manifestation. He did know of these attributes and was glad to be thus conscious. He was placed upon Earth as a volatile spirit to witness certain events of creation, and with his knowledge of Pleasure-Pain he was to rise higher than angels in the system of creation. He was to be given promise of such induction into honorable godhood. He was conscious that he had such destiny, but he lacked, most of all, Patience. His wisdom became his plaything. He broke his covenant with the Father and tried to be God himself too soon, and before his education was complete.

THUS DO YE DERIVE YOUR CONCEPTS OF FALLEN ANGELS AND PURGATORIAL HELL ✣

HE FATHER was not vengeance-given. In His heart He was grieved, for He had planned much good for man. He did not war on impatient man, making mischief with his premature powers of wisdom. He only rebuked man with colossal catastrophe, and handicapped him from making further mischiefs

by taking away his knowledge. Man fell, not from grace, but from divine wisdom into ignorance.

Came I unto this world to restore that dignity, and the wisdom which was lost. Came we to restore men to consciousness of their true relationship with us.

Men responded at once, perceiving their error. Apes though they were in physical form, yet did they walk uprightly and come to know themselves. Apes as animal species knew NOT themselves as themselves. Therein lieth the difference which perplexeth you.

MAN AS SELF-KNOWER REVEALETH HIS DIVINE ORIGIN!

Thus hath the Plan worked out.

Over and over have I visited the world in physical manifestation. Over and over have I been helped and interpreted by you, My servants. Over and over have we raised up patterns for men to live by, and profit by, in their ideals, that they might regain their surrendered godhood ⚸

Know that ye have been my disciples and servants since Time was. Over and over have we conspired together to bring man up from his bestiality and reduce him to clean spirit, fit to ascend and form reunion with the Father. Know that I have been the Inner Spirit of every great religious leader who ever was. Know that ye have been again and again my interpreters unto apes-rising-to-be-gods.

I am Spirit made manifest by Love, seeking My lost

spiritual sheep to herd them back into the fold of My Father, and making man to regain his lost estate AS SOMETHING FIT TO REIGN OVER A HUNDRED THOUSAND MILLON WORLDS THAT HAVE NOT YET TAKEN FORM!

Know that I have seen our work progressing faintly though steadily at times. Know that I have guarded well My trust and now we make the last assault again on the final vestiges of the Beast in man, making him to lay aside his combativity toward his own species.

We are a company in loving conspiracy to help men be as gods through processes of continual rebirth into Pain and Pleasure without admixture of abomination or change in physical species. We are making the Plan succeed by eternal love and patience, but always remembering that man born of woman is prone to darkness from uncountable aeons when he suffered himself to abominate.

This too do I reveal unto you—

KNOW YE THAT IT MARKETH YOU AS SPIRITS OF CHRISTS YOURSELVES THAT YE DO AID ME IN ACHIEVING THIS VAST REDEMPTION IN THE PRESENT!

I tell you it calleth for Christs to live among men in blindness and darkness, yet always awakening in each life experience to the identities making it of moment. Ye have done it before. Ye will do it oft again. Ye are immortal of Soul and Spirit and loving Mission.

Whence think ye cometh otherwise your love for humankind? Humankind hath not this love, each member for the other; only Christ and servants have such love ☨

Mankind contendeth and findeth joy in bargaining and taking profit from his brother; he findeth joy in quarreling for quarreling's sake, for that the Mark of the Beast is upon him still. I tell you, ye are not of good fortune among men who have the Mark, for they do know in their subconscious minds that ye are not as they, and they fear you. So do they traffick with you under duress; they challenge and despoil you; they say, These are our enemies in that they know more than we, therefore let us imprison them and silence them lest their tongues of wisdom do damage to our beasthood ☨

And yet I say unto you, ye are men and women for purposes of facility in discharging your missions. Know ye that if you did come unto earth as superhuman spirits, men would fear you more and slay you, making your errands to have futile issue. Electing to go into flesh and live after the flesh until your maturities, and the time that the execution of your missions openeth, ye do have communion of attention with humankind everywhere. Thus are ye able to perform that which seemeth natural, and yet which I say unto you is unnatural in holy substance.

Ye do enter into flesh as earthly babes and children, to

acquaint yourselves with physical control of organic instruments for delivery of your divine message. Ye are mortal for a time, then do ye become spiritual and eternal. Ye are saints and martyrs even as I have been saint and martyr. Ye die as men die sometimes and even as I died. Ye ascend unto the Father, even as I, having died, ascended.

Great works do come from our labors. Great spirituality descendeth upon the world when we have manifested thus in flesh. Time upon time do we take communion together and observe that mankind profiteth, that the angel within him groweth a little nearer complete release.

Thus do we remedy in love a great error made millions of years ago, yet Time that was but yesterday in reckonings of eternal values.

Know, My beloved relatives in the Father, that I tell you these matters to prepare your minds for further enlightenment. Know that always have we revealed ourselves to one another when the hour reapproacheth for the covenant to be kept.

Now hear Me further . .

SAY unto all of you who do My work, no matter where earthly residence findeth you: Cometh a time in your revelations of identity when ye do know yourselves for the essences ye are. Cometh with such knowledge in your subconscious minds a series of vibrations which disclose you unto myriads of disgruntled or half-developed or partially dead spirits who do hate the Light for that which the Light discloseth them to be; They do gather about you and make tremendous mischiefs, hoping thereby to thwart the missions ye have undertaken for yourselves, and by such process of thwarting, to hold back the development of mankind UNTIL THEY CAN CATCH UP, or to reduce man back to the errors of Abomination that they may have counsel and company in their dilemmas.

Ye are not wholly aware of your own powers as yet to counteract such activities. Become aware of your powers and use them and the enemy retreateth. But these powers can also become wearied from much vigilance, and from much vigilance cometh lethargy. These are the times when the enemy plagueth most, being aware of your mortal or organic weakness.

Your defencelessness in these times, I instruct you, is not dangerous. They are but annoying, for ye do rise above them and stand forth strong in consciousness that such revelations are natural, and your identities true as ye perceive. The enemy whispereth that ye are hoaxed. In your heart of hearts ye know that ye be not hoaxed, else are ye turned aside from Me to commit abomination of conscience and mission. Take no thought to these whisperings, I tell you. Know that always the mood doth pass. Know that event convinceth you that such revelations as these are godlike and God-given until that moment when ye do recall our pact with the Host by your own memories.

I say unto you, beloved, that moment cometh swiftly. ¶ Know ye that the mind of man is handicapped by vain conceits; these in certain earthly situations may be priceless—they are grievous liabilities in treating with Eternity ☆

Earthly men and women were ye until the spiritual revelations started. Spirit-men and spirit-women became ye when the revelations had begun. So came Knowledge unto you with rote, as earthly men would be given such wisdom. Thus goeth it.

Revelation cometh day unto day and night unto night. Think ye no more of yourselves as of earth. Recall yourselves as angels and ministers and saviors, treating with, in, and by, earthly flesh, this our world that needeth us . .

Rest peacefully, My dear ones. Think of these mysteries that I have expounded. When other nights come, I reveal to you more . . .

ON INTO WISDOM

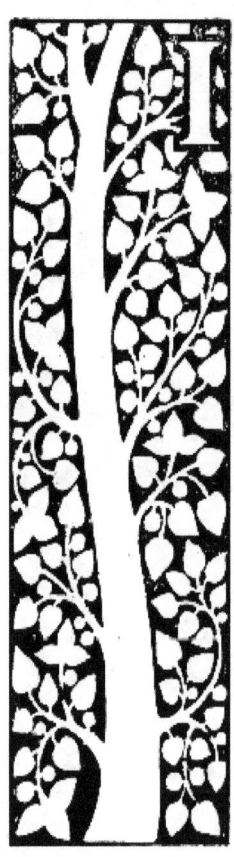

IT MADE sense at last, this orthodox scheme of Salvation, when considered from the premise I transcribed that March night. ¶ Orthodoxy contended that the scheme of salvation arose from the episode of a mythical Eve giving a bit of fruit to her husband Adam, and the two of them eating that which was forbidden. Out of that fantastic fruit-incident—which had wrought an eviction from Eden and thus made men "sinners"—Orthodoxy contended the Perfect Man, Jesus, had to die the death in order to perfect a divine Atonement with the Creator of the worlds. How much more rational and logical was the premise for Redemption laid down in these two surpassing papers:

that man had to be regenerated from his contaminations with vile sodomic forms, lingering in his nature even up to the present? The bestial ingredient in the current human race that is commonly designated as its "animal ancestry" and ascribed to man's evolution from some "common ancestor" with the apes, hasn't been a heritage then, so much as a trespass. Or perhaps the term should be perversion. If he came to this planet back in Oligocene times, in spirit form, just as we are now proposing to attempt interplanetary exploration by jet-driven rocket planes, and created bodily forms for occupancy here in physical sense, and used those forms for copulation with earthly animals, then the Christus mission of winning him back to his original high estate has a substantial and common-sense purpose behind it, and has little or nothing to do with appeasing some mercurial God of Wrath by a blood sacrifice of His own Son. Of course it makes rags of the popular concept of Salvation and Redemption, but it does seem to be far more logical and rational. Salvation and Redemption then become accomplishments stretching over millions of years and embracing all living human entities who have the Beast Heritage in their composition, not just a tiny section of the race that happened to live nineteen hundred years ago at the eastern end of the Mediterranean basin. And eradicating the beast from man, and restoring him spiritually to the creature of angelic status which Divine Intellect originally meant him to be, becomes not a mere proposal of theological doctrine but a vast program of spiritual eugenics. It means putting theology upon a sound ethical basis with the caprices of an anthropomorphic Deity eliminated. The only trouble encountered, in rationalizing it with orthodox doctrine as laid down by the churches of today, is its feature of earthly re-existence.

Earthly re-existence becomes an automatic necessity to execute any such Plan of Salvation as may be based upon winning man from his beastliness, up onto the level of "human angelhood". If these original star guests of Oligocene times created their own thought-forms and employed them for copulation and procreation with earthly forms, it would stand to reason that the similar occupancy of earthly forms today should be equally as possible. Man "goes in and comes out" of these earthly physical forms, century upon century, and millenium upon millenium. Life by life his mortal experiences refine and polish his character, making him more and more spiritual-minded, until the time arrives in the individual case where his "lost" angelic status has been restored. Thereupon he is a fitting candidate for the orthodox "heaven", although there as well we are called upon to raise our sights and consider Heaven in more subliminal aspects. To my way of viewing it, nothing of real value is subtracted from Holy Writ, and the Chief Personage loses none of Its grandeur, but the whole scheme of salvation takes on an enlarged and beautified aspect commensurate with what we are learning in these modern times about the immensity of the universe and the stupendous disclosures of 200-inch telescopes. Every last religious issue, as it were, becomes abruptly magnified to measure up to astronomical findings of the twentieth and twenty-first centuries. It is, in short, a basis for the integrity of the Redemption doctrine that "stands up" under the advancements of the atomic age.

The ancient Hebrews evidently were aware of the antediluvian cosmic facts as to some of the major happenings in the earliest days of the man-race on this planet —obtaining them apparently at second hand from the Osirian mystics, since if they had obtained them at first hand they would have recorded them nearer the premise set forth in the foregoing—but by narrowing their concepts of Divinity down to an anthropomorphic God who fitted the idiosyncrasies of one little tribe of Semitic menials in the big Egyptian picture, they likewise had to make the whole story of Creation and the "Fall" a simple and literal drama that the most childlike among them could understand, all wound around their patriarchal God's tiff at Adam's and Eve's Edenic behavior. Just what Christ had to say about it all when He came along some two thousand years after Moses, we have only limited means for knowing, since it seems evident that plenty of censoring of His more profound expressions went on among the early founders and fathers of the Church, especially the real story behind the significant episode on the Mount of Transfiguration.

Christ seems definitely to have put the stamp of authenticity on Reincarnation—if we stop to give it a moment's thought—when upon coming down from the Mount of Transfiguration He told His disciples in so many words that the souls of Elias and John the Baptist were one and the same. We will go deeper into this further along when we come to probe into the whole process of earthly revisitation. The point I'm trying to make just now is, that considered from any standpoint one little mortal life would be too inanely short for the individual spirit to become salvaged from the beastly acquisitions engendered in the Fall.

That there has been some kind of "Fall" of all humankind from an original high estate, peeps through the disclosures of all orthodoxy on the subject. But too many people, subconsciously desiring exemption—in their own minds at least—want to accept that the only personage who really "fell" was Old Nick himself, taking hordes of unpleasant people along with him. The real Fall of Man as expounded in this psychical research that began on my own part in 1928, would seem more reasonably to boil down to this—

A vast horde of semi-intelligent spirits journeyed through interstellar space some seventeen million years bygone, discovered this earth-planet with its hospitable conditions and indigenous forms of developing biologic life, and decided to stay for a time and live similar lives for educational purposes. They "mixed up" with these indigenous forms of life, got the angel and the earthly interbred in what became Heidelberg or prehistoric man, and created a necessity for physical and spiritual rectification. This rectification started by the Spirit of Christ—or what we know today as the Spirit of Christ—volunteering in consequence of the tragic abomination and attempting to teach and persuade the mongrel spirits to return to their angelhood via the route they had come. It was to be by self-election on the part of each and every individual to weed out the beastly and abominate traits in his own character and return to his original angelic status of his own free will. And this Spirit of Christ had with It, when it appeared on this earth-ball for such purpose, a personal following of Christ People who covenanted with Him to remain here life after life and century after century, and so exemplify the Christ Life and the Christ Teachings that ultimately the whole concourse of original "abominators" should be "saved" . .

So truly we might put it for a working concept, that over the millennia since, there have been three classes or categories of spiritual life maintaining on this solar satellite: first, the indigenous biologic earth-forms that were the Ape Mothers of the original Sodomites; second, the "sons of God" who came via the Great Migration and "looked upon the daughters of earth" and saw

that they were fair and chose of them wives; and third and last, the Christ People who arrived to make a cosmic mission of mentoring the "angelic host that fell" into the practices of mixing the heavenly and earthly breeds, and winning it back to its original angelic status.
¶ The Vicarious Atonement, considered on this premise, doesn't stand up for one moment, of course. One Perfect Man dying for the sins of the world makes a decidedly pretty legend but does no one any benefit of lasting value to his own spirit. People have to stand up to penalties for their own malfeasance in this world, and only as they endure and pay those penalties do they come into consciousness of the erroneous courses of human conduct and their inevitable aftermaths. But that rebellious and disgruntled "fallen angels" should persistently attack and slaughter the Great Avatar, life upon life whenever He appeared in flesh, because they resented His errand of showing them the error of their ways, would be consistent behavior. Pivoting the entire dogma of world-wide religion upon just one such assassination, however, would seem to the erudite to be sheer doctrinal subterfuge.

ONSIDERED as world-wide ethical premise for the Scheme of Salvation, however, this psychical description of the Fall somehow made more sense to me than the squeamishly pragmatic—not to say dogmatic—interpretation that my clergyman-father had proclaimed from his pulpit, via St. Paul, since I had been knee-high to a grasshopper. As the saying goes, it "clicked" . .

It was a relieving discovery to make, I felt, that I had more than one little mortal life to straighten out the kinks in my own spiritual ensemble, that no fiery hell was yawning for me because once in my twelfth year I had looted a neighboring farmer's melon patch and cheated a trusting old lady out of seventy cents, neglected to say my prayers over a whole twelvemonth when a blonde maiden of my acquaintance had departed the town with an older and handsomer male, and refused to attend revival services in the local temple when the "saved of the Lord" gathered to holler their heads off to organ music and pat themselves on their own backs because their futures were all fixed up, and I didn't believe it. I was, in other words, LIVING IN ETERNITY NOW, and had all the time ever to be created in which to come back to earth and straighten myself out physically, mentally and spiritually. Salvation wasn't of my own choosing at an altar built and polished and carpeted and sanctified by the Baptists or the Presbyterians or the Methodists or Seventh-Day Adventists; salvation was of my own choosing because I would eventually sicken of knocking around this old planet with the dumb and coarse progeny of abominations and whoredoms, and "go the right path" because it meant less intellectual trouble and moral complications.

To put it in still more graphic language, what I was being given in the matter of Doctrine over this psychical pencil had the summed-up effect of MAKING JESUS CHRIST A PERSONAGE OF SENSE.

Maybe there had been a time when a great horde of adventuring spirits took off into Cosmos to see what distant worlds were like—atomic experts are considering the possibilities in rockets to the same end today. Maybe they had gotten onto this solar planet along about the times of the Miocene Period and had themselves a grand shindy chasing good-looking female apes up trees —although in all my life I have never seen a good-looking female ape . . not one I'd feel like chasing up a tree at any rate. Maybe it had been necessary for an Avatar to come here and over vast periods indicate to the cosmic adventurers what a lot of viciousness and nonsense they were practicing. At least I wasn't being asked to engage in a plethora of theological controversies that put up my everlasting destiny to the caprices of a superior Being who found the celestial time to hunt up an old sinner by the name of Moses in ancient Midian and predicate the future of society on how he reacted when the bushes caught fire, or how Egypt rained toads when the presiding potentate decided he had his own Houdinis who could rain the toads down better.

I had a doctrine that was sensible and rational being propounded to me, and it behooved me to go as far as I could in it, and gain all the particulars about it that these Invisible Entities elected to give me. Later, when I had it in its entirety, I could endorse it or reject it as I saw fit.

S TIME went on, however, and the weeks and months of manuscript piled up, I realized I was obtaining such a wealth of detail about this mystical origin of the "beast" in man, that I couldn't stop it from becoming the very backlog of my thinking. There was no scientific way, of course, to prove or disprove the occupation of prehistoric ape bodies by spirit entities of a non-earthly order of creation. However, on the other hand I discovered myself in possession of such a perfectly completed hypothesis for the phenomena of conscious life on this planet in all its varied aspects, that the very symmetry and rationality of it seemed to attest to its validity. The doctrine, strange to say, had no bone to pick with either the evolutionist or the theologian, but embraced—or at least reconciled—the basic tenets of both. Biologic forms indigenous to this planet could have built up indeed from chemical components insofar

as organic distinctions were concerned. There COULD have been a Fall of Man in the manner in which the doctrine described—not from anything having to do with a literal Adam and Eve in a worldly garden, eating fruit of a Forbidden Tree but from a transcendent spirit form into gross organic flesh. It was the highest demonstration of altruism that the Great Mentor Spirit, colloquially known to us as the Christ, should have appeared on this bedeviled planet and taken over the job of pulling these "fallen" creatures out of their besottedness, assisted by helpers who made a business of that sort of thing out of pure regard for Him and His sublime ministrations. None of it deprecated or discounted what the New Testament had to say upon the subject of spiritual morals or accomplishments, or the ultimate glories of the human race at the End. All of it gave a certain transcendent dignity to world salvation.

I knew if it helped me as it did with the headaches of orthodoxy, it must have similar effects on others.

In other words, as the Mentors had apprised me in those first few nights in Mary's apartment, the real Celestial Instruction didn't consist of a dour list of Thou-Shalt-Nots, but sensibly and maturely delineated what the Life Proposition was on this planet, and what it could be if enlightenment became general.

I was still mulling over this latest paper on why the great felines had their inexplicable ferocity toward the human race, when the paper "Where Doctrine Came

From" seemed to carry the expositions another step forward. Bear with me while I reprint this paper for your expanding enlightenment—

THE REVELATION

Where Doctrine Came From

MY DEARLY BELOVED:

I TELL you of matters that are goodly to have spoken; I tell you of more mysteries, that ye may be strong in your faith in My divinity; I tell you of the beginnings of Doctrine, of which men have not heard . .

Know that in the Beginning, My beloved, was no form, Intellect WAS; man had no image of physical body. Always was he created spirit by Spirit.

Know ye that Intellect sought flesh for a purpose. Man had no evidence of Self in spirit, meaning Self as identity. Spirit hath no identity as such. Only after long experience on planes of the flesh doth spirit feel itself
This identification cometh through the trial and error of life as mortal being. Mortal meaneth Absolute in Flesh; it meaneth not always Body of Matter.

Flesh is Matter but matter is not always flesh.

Know therefore that man as spirit came into this earth-plane to incarnate for continued earthly experience. Men were to know pain and pleasure through earthly senses and thus gain to knowledge of themselves as separate entities.

Thereupon man made himself to abominate as the Scriptures have informed you. But know that he was

saved by the Host for a purpose: HE WAS TO RULE AS GOD—EACH IN HIS OWN RIGHT—OVER PLANETS NOT YET BORN!
He was to know the power of Creative Thought and be as the Father in lesser mold. He was to have the knowledge of flesh that he might harken to the cries of flesh on planets under his control.

MAN WAS divine from the Beginning, an emanation from the Father, knowing Good and Evil, abstaining from creating that which had no loving purpose. Man, however, embraced his opportunity to make himself god of earth-creation without awaiting the proper experience. Thus did he fill the earth with his Thought Forms.
What think ye is the meaning in the Scriptures of the fiery destruction of Sodom and Gomorrah? Having the monsters with him, did he procreate with them physically and bring upon himself the inevitable catastrophe. There was naught else to be done but to extirpate this wrong in a series of physical and fleshly experiences, that through the overcoming of the weaknesses and desires of his flesh he might be cleansed of that with which he had become contaminated.
Thus do I instruct you.
These earthly visitations have been maturing aeon on aeon, form unto form, body unto body.
Know that since Time was, man hath been created.

That is to say, man hath had existence in Thought Incarnate or Holy Spirit. So too hath all else.

Man hath had no Beginning and shall have no Ending except that he desireth it. Man hath made his own destiny, aeon on aeon. He hath had his planetary habitation shown him. Verily hath he ennobled it or defiled it. Know that he hath made himself Spiritual Abominations even as in the days before Sodom and Gomorrah he made himself physical abominations ☙

Know that those who hate the Light are devolving back into Everlasting Namelessness, while those who love the Light are evolving into everlasting transitions of glory unto glory until they are one with the Perfect Godhead ☙

See ye now why I say unto you that the Father is Thought Incarnate, Holy Spirit?

We too are Thought Incarnate.

Thought IS. Thought WAS. Thought WILL BE.

We are manifesting as Thought Incarnate when we greet one another thus.

Thought is not thinking as men know it, that is, exercising imagings. Thought thinketh only facts as existences, which is profound for your earthly minds to conceive, yet should you grasp it. Now mark this well—

THERE cometh a time in the evolution of man returning to perfect Godhood from physical existence for purpose, when he saith to himself: Lo, the Father maketh us to suffer—not realizing that he maketh himself to suffer for experience, having later utility in his own godhood ⚜

Know that being blind of concept, he looketh upon Nature and saith: Behold I see visions, behold I feel miracles; the least powerful of created things am I, yet behold I see that which hath more meaning than I can interpret for myself.

Whereupon he cometh unto his neighbor and contendeth: Lo, we are as grass in the field; lo, we are as sheep among wolves; lo, we have no resting-place that giveth us security; let us now in our weakness blame God, saying: Father of Creation art Thou, yet dost Thou not make for us any armor of safety from the prowling beast: yet dost Thou not make for us or our children any mode of flight from our enemies. Verily Thou couldst have done these things, and therefore not having done them Thou art transgressor against us.

So saith man to his neighbor and both believe it.

So setteth up man a fort against his fellows in faith and rebuketh the Godhead. So telleth he his misery unto unborn generations and thinketh no further.

Verily is Doctrine born!

Doctrine saith: Behold did our fathers not tell us thus? Wherefore do we, the children, alter our views? Were not our fathers wiser than we, their children?

They forget, My beloved, that experience maketh wisdom. They forget that the fathers have had the shorter

lives; verily the children outlive the parents and wax stronger and wiser; verily the doctrine of the children is wiser, being fecund with the fruits of a wiser observation. Yet do they cling to custom and say: Behold the fathers told us, therefore we do it.
Verily the fathers have not told them. The fathers only saw and spake. The children treasured such speakings, naming them Wisdom. Verily the speakings were as observant meanderings. Lo, the children regard them as of gold. Now let us reason further—

MAN HATH a proness in his spirit to seek wisdom. Verily he longeth for the power of creation which cometh from great knowledge. Knowing ever of his lost Godhood, he doth strive to abominate now in manufacture. This is pleasant unto him as he groweth in stature and cometh nearer and nearer to his original perfection. Yet now he doeth it with Matter clumsily —materials, as ye call them—and not with Spirit cleverly. Cometh a time when he standeth erect and saith: Behold our machines are superfluous! Have we not knowledge of ether? Have we not knowledge of powers of thought? Have we not energy—or vibration? What would we create? All things hereby exist. Let us make as we desire, having the factors thereof ☙
¶ I tell you that in that day man shall have regained his lost divinity and we who shall have taught him shall be as freers of slaves. It is our joy that we are makers

of gods for worlds that shall in turn rise and fall and be of blind concept. Into eternal space, aeon on aeon, and into eternal time, light-year on light-year, shall we make manifestation ⚜

KNOW THAT EVEN I, YOUR WISER ELDER BROTHER, HAVE NO KNOWLEDGE OF THE EXTENT TO WHICH WE RISE!

Thus do we come to the kernel of our discourse . .

Man hath made much progress into the infinite. Man hath challenged us and we have smiled. Man hath been of good and bad report and we have indulged him. Man hath made graven images and worshiped them. Verily he hath been as a child worshiping human parent. Man hath an itching after eternal thought and maketh the tool which enableth him to protect himself against his adversary. Whereupon he saith: Behold this God whom we blamed for not creating us with armor is not important. We arm ourselves; we make our own armament; therefore is He superfluous. We have no need of Him, having protection now from those who would run us down.

Thus reasoneth man stronger with each new invention, not knowing all the time that he is part of the body of the Father—Thought Incarnate—Holy Spirit—which maketh such inventions or alloweth them to come to pass in materials.

Man riseth higher and higher. Lo, he needeth the Father more than ever, FOR BY THE FATHER HE RISETH!

NOW KNOW ye, My beloved, that man hath secretly a knowledge of his identity and his power. He knoweth that he is not a brute. He feareth that he is god, yet lacking divine attributes which gods must own he swayeth to and fro in his imaginings and becometh as one tongue-tied at his own limitations. He seeketh out God in his closet and saith: Father-Creator, give unto me the power that I may manifest correctly. He seeketh out God in assembly and saith: Give us power O Great Jehovah, that we may fall upon those we hate, and slay them!

Verily all masses do this. They are fearful of one another separately, yet coming together en masse do they hate. They are fearful separately and distrust en masse. I say unto you, beloved, they shall have this order of their beseechments reversed. When they do foregather and pray: Father, let us manifest together to Thy glory, meaning it in their hearts, then shall they draw each man into his closet and pray: Father, be merciful unto me for mine weakness!

Now I come unto you with yet profounder knowledge:

MAN HATH made unto himself an Image of Hope which he worshipeth. He saith in his heart, Lo, we have knowledge of an order which pointeth upward. Whence came such knowledge? Came it from ourselves? . . verily we would know it. Therefore it cometh from other planes of spirit. Such planes are not of us, therefore are favors extended to us. Mayhap we merit such favors further, or mayhap further favors are lying in wait which we know not of. Therefore let us prove worthy that they may come to us.

I say unto you, beloved, that faith hath wrought miracles from just such reasonings. Verily the Father manifesteth therein. Verily Thought Incarnate, the Holy Spirit, thus ennobleth its recipient.

Man hath gone far with Doctrine. He hath permitted abomination of intellect. Truth he hath made mock of. He hath cleansed his house of perverted things also. He hath embraced goodly hopes. Thus do we love him, for have we not struggled in the dark ourselves? He hath made goodly progress and our happiness in him is warranted. But let Me tell you more—

Man hath come to that place where intellect hath seized him and said unto him: Behold you go forth as a lion proudly, knowing well your strength. Ye have concept of traps and therefore ye do fear them not. Ye do stalk your preys with cunning.

Harken, My beloved, . . Intellect betrayeth.

Intellect saith to a man: Thou art wise beyond thy generation. God saith to a man: Be humble in thy wisdom for verily ye lose it easily.

This is My converse with you, beloved. Think ye not of favors shown. Know that My love is your favor. Share it with the multitude that our work may be done!

DISCARDING FEAR

DISCARDING FEAR

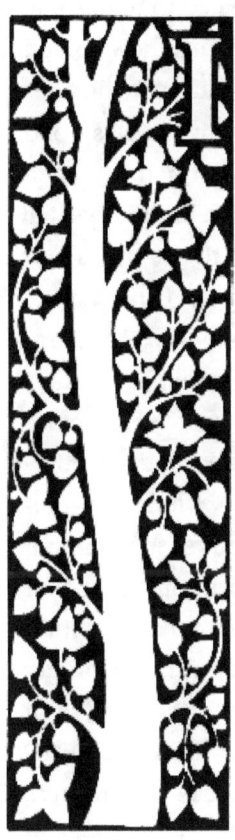IT STANDS to reason that if you begin young enough with a human being, instill the thought into his intellect as an unassailable truth that somewhere beyond the gates of death there is a fiery region in which he will land if he fails to accept the pronouncements of dogma he is always going to be disconcerted by the worry that he is running a hazard to explore fresh ideas and teachings respecting the Hereafter for himself ⁋ We get so-called religious notions into our heads at an infantile and formative age, and when we gain to adulthood we feel a vague subconscious distress if anything is introduced to us that appears at variance with them. This is particularly true if the anxiety

creeps in, that entertaining fresh concepts is any species of "sin" . . We have an instinctive desire not to "sin", if we be reasonably law-abiding temperaments, but if our minds are automatically shut and sealed against fresh knowledge by past religious instruction, we are fated to live and think from a bed of Procrustes. The mental condition of the average person seems to have it that all religious truth was revealed to man some twenty centuries ago, that there is nothing new to add without it being "wickedness", that the universe makes no progress in spiritual wisdom, and "what was good enough for the fathers is good enough for us." Then when we make the twentieth-century discovery that spiritual wisdom evolves and expands the same as any other wisdom, and that the Fathers by no means had any monopoly on the eternal verities, we are introduced to confusion. It isn't that God changes in character or essence from age to age but that we as more capable mental beings grow in our capacities to interpret and comprehend Him. With the whole race advancing in intellectual capacity as it moves into the potentialities of the atomic age, my contention has it that no one can ever "sin" by assiduously pursuing the hunt for Truth. After all, the truth IS the truth, no matter who gets a revelation of it—or in what race or time or tongue. Christ couldn't talk about the horrors of warfare waged with atomic bombs because his hearers wouldn't have known what he was discussing—even guns hadn't been evolved in His day, to say nothing of any kind of bombs. But that wouldn't mean that Jesus knew nothing about the possibilities for destruction in the fission of atoms, or that atoms wouldn't have exploded just as readily in the Palestinian era as they did in the World-War II era over Hiroshima, had the mechanics of fission been discovered and operated. It isn't atomic fission that "progressed" between Jesus' time and ours; it is our own scientific acumen. And what applies to the fission of atoms applies equally to the fission of later-day ideas . .

We have been taught for two thousand years theologically that an anthropomorphic God created the first man and the first woman in a literal Garden of Eden, that the pair misbehaved concerning God's specific instructions about eating the fruit of the Tree of Knowledge, and suffered eviction and nakedness as the result. The whole thing happened some four to six thousand years ago, according to Holy Writ, regardless of the fact that we are unearthing political records of Sumerian dynasties that affect to go back 435,000 years. God came down from His heaven and rebuked the two for their disobedience, sent them forth as nude wanderers on the surface of the earth, and held a divine grudge against their species and progeny until Christ came to earth and died as the Sinless Man, which made everything right. Nobody knew much about the vast astronomical universe, back in the Palestinian times in which this so-called "holy" writ was compiled. People accepted a simple story of Original Sin and Vicarious Atonement as the last word in Eschatology, and all celestial inquiry ceased. If it didn't, someone got taken out and had a "holy" bonfire built around his feet. The biblical Jehovah was personal Lord of this planet—which was the center of the universe—and the other heavenly bodies were mere "lights" hung upon the veranda ceiling of the universe. The whole thing was a sort of "country-village" concept of celestiality, and any city slicker who came around with notions of vaster concepts was an emissary of the Evil One. Now with the whole earth becoming filled up with city slickers, insofar as knowledge of astronomy and physics applies, we commence to scrutinize orthodoxy for its profounder and more essential truths. It is the difference, of course, between spiritual sophistry and academic provincialism.

In other words, just as men once upon a time supposed the inhabited regions around the Mediterranean to contain all the humanity and civilization that existed on the planet—or that amounted to a kopeck—only to discover later that the world held five continents each with its peculiar type of mortal life, so man in his intellectual and cultural advance today has to adjust himself to the disclosure that there are other worlds and planetary systems, and undoubtedly other humanities and cultures, all contained in the immensity of Cosmos and all probably of as much importance in Divine Mind as anything of seeming moment here on the planet Earth. Discovering that the universe is a million—or a billion—times more sizable than anything remotely imagined by the early fathers of theology, doesn't alter basic aspects of Truth, however. Holy Spirit as divine originator of all stars, suns, solar systems, and probably the sentient life on planets, is no less significant for having created a million planets, is no less awesome and respect-commanding, and that Its presence and performance has been going on for four thousand million years instead of four thousand years, doesn't alter the nature of First Causes. The First Causes in all their aspects and performings are Truth, and it is purely the mark of spiritual maturity to be able to grasp it in its magnitude. To say that it is "sinning" to examine into Truth in whatever aspects it can be comprehended, is to glorify ignorance and exalt illiteracy. It is putting a premium on spiritual adolescence and scorning wisdom as synonymous with evil.

The facts seem to have it—and we had better admit it no matter how much our little mortal vanities feel offended—that the planet Earth is only one of thousands and perchance millions of similar worlds on which conscious life is developing, all of it equally as valuable in the eyes of Divine Spirit, and it devolves upon us to achieve to a spiritual hypothesis that rationalizes the entire celestial ensemble, not one little third-rate planet revolving about a sixth-rate sun in a far "northern" corner of the whole stellar galaxy. The facts are the facts, and the truth about the universe is going to remain the truth about the universe, no matter how awed or irked we show ourselves in reaction to our perturbing unimportance.

ALK OUT under the clear heavens on a summer's night and something like 2,000 stars are visible to your unaided vision. Buy a three-inch telescope, costing at the most a few hundred dollars, and the number of distant suns observable jumps to more than 200,000 while with the great photographic telescopes in the standard observatories the number jumps again to more than 400 millions!

Which, we might ask ourselves, is the truth about the heavens: the 2,000 stars we can see with our naked eyes—as the ancients saw them about the time that our Holy Writ was compiled—or the 200,000 to be seen with a three-inch telescope, or the 400 millons seen by the photographic telescopes? Any intelligent person replies, of course, that the truth lies in the 400 millions. And yet that mayn't be the truth any more than the 2,000 discernible with the naked eye, because we haven't come yet to the maximum construction of telescopes that "see" to the very edges of Infinity. Maybe there aren't any "edges" to Infinity. Maybe the greater the construction, the greater the revelations.

Maybe that as long as we can go on improving telescopes, just so long may we go on discovering millions and billions of more worlds.

Understand, I say MAYBE, and the suggestion is my own. But the thought I'm trying to register in all this is, reaching out mentally and spiritually for Truth Itself is the thing that counts, and the grandeur of it is apparently only circumscribed by our own capacity to discern it.

We are called by the responsibility of our own development to leave the little Hebraic conception of Jehovah-God back in the perception-category with the 2,000 visible stars, and strike out into the unexplored universe of divine ideas to form our concepts of Holy Spirit as It is, with the aid of photographic telescopes in mental observatories. And the history of mortal kind on our own little earth-ball must fit into its proper place in the vast cosmic picture. So too must our hopes and our fears and our aspirations and our personal anxieties—if we have them.

As I have said in "Thinking Alive", when we inspect the heavens on any clear evening, we know that the star-suns we see glinting above us, each differ in brilliance. The brighter ones are either closer or hotter, and we divide this brightness into Magnitudes. There are only 20 stars of first magnitude and they are 2,512 times as bright as those of second magnitude, while those of third magnitude are only 2,512 as bright as

those of second magnitude—and so on down the list. We can't see stars of less than the sixth magnitude with the naked eye and the faintest within reach of our most modern telescopes are in the seventeenth magnitude.
¶ Sirius, I say again, is the brightest of all the stars. Others of first magnitude are Arcturus, Vega, Capella and Procyon. The North Star, and those in the design of the Big Dipper, are stars of the second magnitude, while those in the mystical little group we call the Pleiades are of fourth magnitude. The inherent brilliance of these stars differs greatly, millions of them being bigger and brighter than our sun. Some of them are from one hundred to two hundred times brighter than our sun, the stars in the Big Dipper and the Pleiades for example. Others are thousands of times as great as our sun in sheer light-giving power—Rigel and Canopus for instance. And these star-suns are all so remote that the distances between them can only be determined with the greatest difficulty. Alpha Centauri is the nearest star-sun to us and yet it wasn't till 1840 that its relative distance was measured and found to be 275,000 times the distance of our earth from Old Sol—which last is 92,000,000 miles, as every schoolchild knows.
One famed astronomical writer puts it: Perhaps the remoteness of the stars from one another can best be understood from the fact that there is, on an average, only one star to about four units of stellar space, and one unit of stellar space is a sphere whose radius is

206,000 times the distance of the earth to the sun, or in round numbers, twenty thousand million miles. Even in the great globular star clusters, in which the telescope reveals from 5,000 to 50,000 suns in a part of the sky no bigger than that covered by the disk of the moon, the average distance of those stars is 50,000 times the 92 million miles between the sun and the earth.

Our own position and size in the celestial system is so small and insignificant that if a general map of Cosmos could be drawn, even our sun wouldn't be marked on it at all and our earth would scarcely be known to exist. At the most, our sun would be regarded as an unimportant fleck by comparison with a majority of the heavenly bodies. Betelguese in Orion is so vast as a star-sun that Old Sol and all of its eight planets in their orbits could be put within the spherical dimensions of it. All of these things constitute astronomical truths that must be faced—theology or no.

To say that with 400 million suns in the sky, some of them 335 as big and hot as our own, none of them has planets similar to earth, on which spirit-life has come into performance, would seem to be talking absurdities. We would seem to be faced, on this earth—by the sheer logic of astronomical possibilities—with a religious condition premised on well-nigh prehistoric ignorance. To assume that God in the form of a glorified patriarch, creator of such stupendous magnitude, could possibly come to take sides, so to speak, between Israelites and Gentiles, or harbor personal resentments against individuals on such a sixth-rate little earth-ball, is to treat with nothing less than sacrilegious fantasy. Almost, we might put it, the first step in the determination of Truth is to get ourselves and our planetary residence into the right perspective with the rest of the universe. It is the part of common sense.

We can credit in all seriousness, just the same, that despite the relatively small size of our planet, as planets go, and its general cosmic inconsequence, it MIGHT make the soundest kind of sense that millions of years in the past a horde of celestial discarnates did find this particular satellite of Old Sol's whirling about the sun, with biologic life developing upon it built up from chemical origins, and settled down upon it and interbred with that life, precipitating a spiritual situation that called for a "Redemption" under mentorship of a Christus. It is, to say the least, something rational to consider ⁂

But when you stop to give it thought, there is something just as rational in the fact that the only scheme of Redemption that would make sense on that premise, would be one in which a person lived more than one physical life.

Stop with me a moment in this earnest hunt for Truth, and consider what would happen if a new soul were created for all eternity each time a given pair of parents had progeny. The compounding of numbers is a terrific thing, and one not to be disregarded in biology any more than elsewhere. We get into utterly fantastic incalculables when we consider mortal life as having originated with Adam and Eve in a Garden of Eden . .

ELIEVE-IT-OR-NOT Ripley, the cartoonist, published a book in 1929 in which he called attention to the astronomical figures involved in this matter of compounding human offspring. I quote from Ripley: "Of course you expect to go to heaven when you die. We all do. The hope is in all of us that when we die we will go to some celestial place where we rejoin the other members of our family who have passed onward. But take my advice. Make a reservation! Heaven is becoming very crowded and it is extremely doubtful whether you can get in. Should you manage to squeeze yourself through the Pearly Gates, it is even more doubtful whether you could find the members of your family among the crowd already in possession of the place.

"We will say that you go to heaven and meet your father and mother, not to mention the rest of your kith and kin. When you meet your father and mother, they will be with their father and mother, for they would have the same desire to be with their parents that you have to be with yours. And their parents in turn would be with their parents, and so on back through the countless generations of mankind. So you will have to meet them all. You cannot be snooty in heaven, you know, and snub anybody.

"Now if we take 25 years as a generation, we find that there have been 77 generations since the time of Christ. And if we count only your parents, their parents, and so on backward for that length of time, we find that you must meet 302,231,454,903,657,293,676,543 relatives—all different. OUR OWN LITTLE WORLD WOULD NOT HOLD THAT STUPENDOUS NUMBER! If that many people were on earth today, they would have to be stacked up on each others' heads! Allowing them two square feet to stand on, this would make a stack of one solid mass of folks 113,256 miles high all over the earth's surface!

"Suppose you wanted to say 'Hello!' to your dear old grandfather who happened to be located some 113,000 miles up the heap. Of course you would have to climb —there would be no other way except to scramble up this human beanstalk like little Jack. Let us assume that you climbed one-half as fast as the United States Army marches—which is 15 miles a day. If you climbed at the rate of eight miles a day, you would reach your dear old grandpappy about 39 years later—provided you didn't get yourself knocked off meanwhile for stepping on somebody's ear in the ascent. Naturally you will be able to slide down faster and you should reach your own place in heaven 50 years after you left it. That is only two generations—which means that your children, and some of your children's children, will have squeezed in and been looking around for you. You really couldn't expect anybody to hold your place for you for 50 years, so don't be surprised if you are out all around and not able to find your own children anywhere—which means that you will have one hell of a time in heaven.

"Mind you, the above figures do not include brothers, sisters, aunts, uncles, nieces, nephews, cousins, and other relatives. Also, I'm allowing for only 1928 years, although scientists tell us that man has been on earth for countless generations before that time—some estimate it as 100,000 to 17,000,000 years. And since science has proved so conclusively that you are related to all animals with four legs or a long tail that have lived on this earth for the past 100,000,000 years, you will have to include them too. They are all your ancestors! As a social proposition the hereafter appears to be a bit embarrassing . .

"St. John records the limits of heaven in Revelations XXI, 16: ' . . He measured the City with the reed, twelve thousand furlongs. The length, and the breadth, and the height of it were equal.'

"Twelve thousand furlongs is 7,920,000 feet, and when cubed, this is equal to 496,793,088,000,000,000,000 cubic feet. In other words, heaven as visualized by St.

John is about 1,500 miles long in each dimension. If you allow 10 cubic feet as ample space for a human being, you will find that heaven can hold about the following number of persons—49,679,308,800,000,000,000—if packed in tight. This calculation does not allow for the streets of gold or the trees of marvelous leaves and fruits, or the 'pure river of water of life, clear as crystal, proceeding out of the throne of God and of the Lamb.'

"It is apparent that heaven was filled up several hundred years ago—or about the time that Columbus was discovering America. What to do? Obviously there is but one way out. You must die sometime, and since it is so evident that you cannot go to heaven, where shall you go? . . . You said it!"

ACETIOUSLY offered, all this, perhaps. Nevertheless this eternal manufacture of new human beings with, and by, each new generation, holds its mathematical imponderables—assuming that there is an eternal manufacture of new human beings with, and by, each new generation. Supposing there isn't!

When these Sages of the Invisible tell us that earthly revisitation is one of the basic facts of life, we can reasonably visualize the physical parents of each new generation merely gestating new biologic bodies for returning spirits to occupy. There are some 2 billion persons thus performing on this planet at the present census of the world's population—almost equally divided as between men and women. Suppose there were another two billion in the Thought Planes. If these four billion souls alternated in their locations or conditions, century after century, there would be no such absurdity of pyramided massings of spiritual human beings on any plane. The same individual spirit-souls could come back into physical occupancy again and again. The thing makes sense.

Of course the fundamentalist comes back with the answer—or explanation—that only a precious few of the "saved" gain to heaven, in proportion to those who are consigned to the Bad Place. But that is neither answer nor solution. If it isn't the fundamentalist's heaven that is overcrowded as per Ripley's calculations, then it must be hell.

Maybe that is why it is hell—because it is so overcrowded on the human beanstalk basis. But it is difficult to credit. If there is no re-existence in the mortal state, then Holy Spirit certainly has installed a somewhat formidable program for the eternal and incessant manufacture of souls. Any box-factory girl and truck-driving boy can get together, with or without benefit of clergy, and proceed to embarrass God with new spirits that must be "judged" at death, and eternally disposed of, whether God wishes to give the judging-time to the progeny or not.

And that's another orthodox absurdity . . the question of "judgment" following the ups and downs of life in this mortal vale of tears.

THERE ARE, all over this world, according to the vital statistics of all civilized countries, 68 deaths a minute, 97,920 daily, 35,740,800 annually—and again I'm indebted to Ripley for my figures. According to Biblical attestments, both the pious and the wicked all come to judgment. But we seem to be bothered by the embarrassing little certainty that there are only sixty seconds of time in any one moment. If 68 deaths occur per minute, that means by common school arithmetic that each soul precipitated into the divine courtroom to be judged for all the temptations and involvements of the flesh, gets less than one second of God's time to have his life's history reviewed and his eternal fate meted out to him.

What sort of an equitable review of his life's history would that be, that had to be compressed into less than one second? And furthermore, if the Almighty—no less a Personage would answer—had to pass sentence to eternal bliss or eternal woe on 35,740,800 souls per year, when would He have time to do anything else? And this rate of new prisoners arriving outside the celestial portals to be "judged" keeps on year after year without surcease or let-up, remember, . . and has been keeping up over the whole 1950 years since Jesus was on earth. Does anyone particularly envy the job God once set for Himself by creating Adam and Eve and promising that their good or bad deeds should be reviewed at life's seventy-year termination?

No, the trouble with the early compilers of the text that now constitutes the Bible was an insufferable blindness to the embarrassment of numbers—not to mention an appalling ignorance concerning the quantities of people that existed in the world and the statistics on their demises. They overlooked the eternal Niagara of souls —on the parental manufacturing basis—that would keep on irresistibly, millennium after millennium, without let-up or relief until all the planetary bodies in all the universe were not only crawling with life but piling hundreds of miles up into the air—the biggest heaven and the roomiest hell included. The compounding of numbers is a terrific thing, once it gets out of hand. We all know the old mathematical anecdote of the employer who asked the employe which he would rather receive for the month's work, a stated sum at the end of the month, or a cent a day, the sums to be doubled at the end of each day. The first day he was to get one cent, the second day two cents, the third day four cents, the fourth day eight cents, and the fifth day sixteen cents. At the end of the first week he would have earned 64 cents, and at the end of the second week $79.36. But by the end of the third week the amount compounded to $10,158.08, and when the 30 days had run, the employer would have owed the employe the stupendous sum of $5,200,936.96. Do your own figuring if you're skeptical about it. Now let's say that instead of pennies doubling, it's the original Adam and Eve in the Garden of Eden, and instead of the time element of days, suppose we substitute generations. Give Adam and Eve four children, two to replace themselves and two for increase. Let these four grow to maturity and have eight, and these eight grow to maturity and have sixteen. Let them all live in some location, either on earth or in heaven or in hell. The compounding of such increase would represent such numbers of people —originating or gestating on this earth-planet only, remember—that the whole solar system couldn't contain them, assuming they maintained the same corporal dimensions they displayed in physical life. And with all these incomprehensible numbers of souls expecting to receive individual "judgment" the project of divinity becomes in turn unthinkable.

The fundamentalist might reply that God being what He is, He could do it by some method outside our present knowledge, even outside the factor of Time. But nowhere in all the sacred lore we possess is there the faintest reference to the phenomenon of God either enlarging or telescoping Time or conducting cosmic business on any other basis than the one that operates in the most prosaic and practical of our worldly affairs.

In fact, our prosaic and practical tempo of worldly affairs is Holy Spirit in action on this plane. And right at the start we discover the contentions of orthodox eschatology utterly defeated and driven to rout by numbers. All of it seems to be the psychological reflexes of a roster of early writers who supposed that all the mortal denizens of creation were represented by the populations of the countries immediately around the eastern end of the Mediterranean Basin. They had no comprehension—those early writers—of the numbers of created souls in other parts of the earth, or if they thought they did, they got rid of the annoyance of them by saying that the others born and living outside the chosen faith, died the death at the end of the mortal span, perished to stay perished, and were never again heard from. A fine way to solve such a problem!

Self-preservation being one of the prime laws of Nature, if not the first, a vast catalog of Fear complexes was compiled around the performances of getting born, and living, and worshiping, and dying out of the body. That vast indescribable Fear mania is something that all but a little group of the Enlightened seem to have brought down over the generations with them, and into the present ☸

Apparently it proved easier for the earliest progenitors of religion to scare people into being good—or what passed for being good—than to try to get at, and expound, the basic facts Behind Life.

Y SEPARATING the spiritual and the physical, however, and examining the possibility that the physical may in no wise be responsible for the creation of our immortal spirits, the whole mathematical absurdity of creation alters—or rather, clears. By crediting that spirit is only created by Holy Spirit, that we are all emanations of the Divine First Cause that have come upon this planet at some time in the past and been inhabiting and reinhabiting physical envelopes of organisms to get pleasure-pain experiences for our cosmic educations, we find something presented to our intellects that we can healthily, sanely, and profitably masticate as mental food. A given number of spirits came into the earth's influence and decided to tarry and "have fun" with the biologic forms that were coming to evolutionary maturity upon this terrestrial body. They sank to unspeakable depths of depravity in their sodomic experimentings and had to be ransomed from the unhallowed karma of it. A highly developed Avatar like Jesus, in almost incomprehensible compassion for these irresponsible adventurers, agreed to come among them on an earth-sojourn and re-educate them in customs and manners of moral thinking until they had regained their original divinity of quality. And this was the REAL salvation.

Well, ever since I began to receive the fundamentals of it, I found it more reasonable to consider and examine than the inequitable proclamation of Adamic sin and Vicarious Atonement. And as I went on and on, with the weeks and months adding up to years, learning more and more of the rational details, I had to conclude that the Higher Sages had something that the orthodox fundamentalists did not.

For one thing, I could consider the Re-Existence Plan of Salvation dispassionately and without the duress of impelling Fear entering in, and really acquire the intellectual tranquility to examine this sweeter and more logical scheme of celestial "redemption" on its merits. In other words, the wisdom that most certainly was coming to me from Somewhere wasn't trying to terrorize me into being rectitudinous; it put the proposition of what had assertedly happened on this earth, in front of me, and asked me to investigate it and pass judgment on it in terms of its lasting and comforting profit to my spirit. And when I not only found Genesis, but the eschatology of all ancient religions and "mysteries" rich with fundamental references to the abortive behaviors of early denizens of this planet, I had to decide that the most vital and significant parts of the Plan of Salvation had been deleted from Christology in order to avoid controversies over earthly return and its accompanying responsibilities and present the more acceptable but fantastic Paulist thesis of Salvation by Grace. Somebody had been spiritually political!

Be that as it may, however, when the wisdom of my

Sages presented what seemed to be a factual picture in which I could discover neither discrepancies nor illogicisms, my own practical nature converted me to the rationalities of my own doctrine, and began to convert others to the degree to which I shared it.

The big thing in it, appealing to me, was that I didn't have to apologize to the basic faith of Christianity for anything I got out of it. The plan of a practical salvation was in it, but minus a mercurial God of Wrath—Whom I never really had believed existed anyhow—and I didn't require a fear of hell-fire breathing down my neck to make me give it attention and assiduously explore it. Furthermore, whatever this "undeleted" doctrine came to propound, seemed to fit in miraculously with all the more recent findings of astronomy, biology, and physics. In the language of the man in the street, "everything was taken care of;" there weren't many loopholes that required plugging up by the orthodox recourse of ascribing to the Power of God anything and everything that was otherwise non-understandable.

¶ So I wanted most of all to know all I could obtain about the tenets of Re-Existence. And for weeks, it seemed, the Sages who were thus indulging me, patiently dictated scores of papers and lectures on the subject. Many of them, perhaps, should more properly be published in my next succeeding volume, "Adam Awakes", but it's all the one doctrine that's being delineated and if you don't get it in the one book, before we're finished you'll get it in the others. I got it more or less "hit or miss" as I propounded questions occurring to me and had answers returned me befitting my inquiries 🌿

But one thing the doctrine did do for me unquestionably . . it demolished all religious Fear for me.

First of all, it removed all terror of dying from me. It proposed a simple, logical, kindly program of being given ample opportunity again and again in physical flesh to perfect myself and achieve my ideals without being "jumped" every few minutes, or days, or years, by an old fuss-budget of a Deity who was watching me for moral transgressions as a cat might watch a mouse. Holy Spirit, I came to realize, had better business, and more important business, in this stupendous Cosmos where the nearest neighboring sun was 275,000 times 92,000,000 miles from us, than peeping through the mortal blinds, hours without end, to see how I was behaving privately and whether I was violating any of the Paulist codes of conduct that jeopardized my eternal bliss. I had my salvation in my own hands, so to speak, and if I did the wrong thing it brought its own penalties reactively right on the spot and in its own coin. If I did wrong to certain individuals in this mortal world, I had lives without end to meet those people anew and rectify my blunders and unkindnesses. I could build my own salvation according as I made definite choice between right and wrong modes of conduct year by year. I was, in other words, constructing my own Day of Judgment—or forging my own judgment—as I lived along, and God wasn't obliged to waste His divine time allotting me four-fifths of a second for a post-mortem "trial" to see whether I belonged among the harp-players or the pitch-shovelers. I got emotional emancipation out of it if I got nothing else.

O, ON this premise I take you along with me through expositions of the Doctrine as it persistently accrued to me. You may not believe a word of it, and no Gates of Hell will yawn for you if you reject it. It is by no means a doctrine that terrorizes mortals into being moral. These things occurred and are going on re-occurring. You see the manifest evidences of them on every side. Paulist orthodoxy can't explain them, and makes no attempt to expound them. But the rise and fall of systems and empires today is rationalized by the teachings of my subliminal sages, and the ups and downs of humanity religiously accounted for. You come to know why you are WHAT you are, and "how you got that way" in the first place.
A philosophy that does this, I claim, is worthy of our most august attention and inquiry.
Now let's see, to illustrate, what some of the most interesting major papers on these subjects contain to tell us further—

THE REVELATION

More about Earthly Return

THE STREAM of Life flows on unending from age to age, from planet to planet, from universe to universe. Within this mighty stream is Love, and Harmony, and Joy. WITH this mighty stream flows power unlimited and life eternal. Each molecule, each spirit particle is borne along by the power of the Everlasting Stream, and when it is truly conscious of that stream, all its little puny effort is to go along more harmoniously upon its destined route. If, however, it is unaware of its nature and its destiny, it sometimes struggles to pit its helplessness against that irresistible force, and is bruised and buffeted until it finds Truth.

Now this Stream is made up of succeeding waves of Cause and Effect. In his earliest visits to earth, each spirit particle that became man as you know him in present physical form, set in motion certain Causes that had to, someday, have their Effects. These were swept into the main current of the Stream and carried forward to times of fruition. It is so in every case. Every man's case is different as to individual traits and their performings, based on his experiences—and of course what we say goes for women as well—and yet all men's cases are the same in this: They must always reap in some analogous form the harvests which they have sown as seed 🕊

This main current of the Stream of Life thus carries with it all the smaller streams of human destiny, and the multitudinous streams of all the individual human destinies that are the incarnations of Spirit in the earth-plane. So there is no stopping the stream of Life and Destiny. There is only the opportunity for beating back and forth and trying to swim against it instead of with it.

After any given earth-cycle has been entered upon, the ever-evolving and climbing spirit begins to see the effects of earlier causes that have conditioned it in what it finds itself, but it also begins to set in motion new causes, some of which bear more or less immediate fruit and some of which must go along into still later life cycles.

When any spirit is existing on what we call—for want of a better term—the Thought Plane between each cycle, it sees with remarkable clearness this chain of Cause and Effect. But if it carried that knowledge consciously with it into each new body, it would possess such power that it would not learn the lessons it is supposed to learn by entering upon that sequence. When it is approaching the end of its sequences in mortality, it is sometimes given conscious glimpses into its past— the phenomenon of what you call Lifted Memory. This may even amount to actual memory, if the climbing soul is faithful and the phenomenon serves some constructive purpose and not merely idle curiosity.

So when you say that life is a matter of foreordination, you are right within certain limits. That is, you are free to follow or not to follow, whatever you have for a light, and you can make your destined pathway shorter, though you cannot alter its direction. If you follow the Light, if you accept the working out of Effects from Causes, and endeavor to set in motion new causes that are constructive and not destructive, then you are in harmony with the Master Stream and the irresistible power of the current is with you, and all about you, and there is no limit to your progress excepting your own unawareness of the power that is yours.

When your vibrations are in harmony with the Vibrations of Spirit, and you are therefore conscious of your own Stream of Destiny as well as the Master Stream within which it flows, you give your spirit and mind and body completely up to its strength—although this is by no means saying that you drift. You do not drift. You progress with the stream and aided by the stream. You do not drift any more than the steamboat drifts that is "running with the current" . .

OUR GREAT Teacher seems to doubt many times whether or not He is justified in His sacrifice to redeem a world that cares so little for His love. He is gratified, nevertheless, by the love of the few who show their devotion by their behavior, but the great mass of the world's populace is infinitely indolent and calloused. There are those who go through scores and scores of lives and still have no use for compassionate love. They are those who use their great talents to cause uprisings against Holy Spirit in all manner of forms. It does not matter that they are "old as the hills", as the saying goes, when it comes to devotion or lack of devotion. You cannot make a man love by giving him age!

The true followers of Christ, especially those Sons of God who have been with Him in this worldly sojourn from the Beginning, keep their hearts open to light, for by it and from it comes their very intellectual and emotional essence. But there are the old sodomic spirits who have never opened their hearts to light, and lived, and still live, because they delight in darkness as a cover for evil deeds. You ought not to worry about them overly much, however, for they are merely injuring themselves. If Our Lord loves them and yet cannot save them—because salvation of any true sort is forever self-salvation—do not feel badly because you cannot do more.

THERE is no way by which you can accurately understand the meaning of Vibration until you come onto the Thought Planes to stay for a session between your earth lives. That it is a potent force for communication between all planes of life is about all that we can tell you at this point of your re-instruction.

The Laws of Spiritual Harmony must be interpreted, we might put it, by some sort of agent, and Vibration acts as an intermediary between the Universe of Spirit and the Universe of Matter.

Vibration may likewise be an attribute of Matter, although not the same as radiation. The composition of the electric granule is not what your men of science today believe. You cannot assemble Matter and have it cohesive unless you have some force that supplies shape and continuity of character. Vibration may do that.

Behind each particle of Matter there is movement toward continual contact with Universal Spirit, that is the essence of Vibration. You have the same principle in Electricity. It is not Matter and yet it affects Matter.
¶ The ways of Creation are strange but they are not inconceivable. If you follow their principles closely you will observe that much of the phenomena that puzzles Science can be traced to this same Vibratory source. It is not Spirit so much as Spirit-in-Operation, and when you are nervous, worried, or doubting, you cause wrong currents of this force to be unleashed and

mixed with that of the eternal and irresistible Cosmos. ¶ You are creating spirit-manifestations of your own, without responsibility and without harmony!

The result is chaos of a sort, not consistent with eternal principles. But do not try to understand this just now. Try to swim, each one of you, with the Great Current of Love, and all things will be revealed in their due order

The way of understanding of these matters is the way of peace and harmony in your whole entities. As you have no cause to question the matters that have already been disclosed to you, so you have no cause to question that in time you will be made wise beyond your generation

There is only one way to receive the gifts that are eternal and therefore priceless: Give unto God the things that are God's, and undertake nothing that is inconsistent with your divine revelations.

Whenever you feel the overwhelming power of Tenderness, know then that He is in communion with you and is knowing the Joys of Brotherhood in the Spirit with you. You are all of you drawing close to Him when you have in your hearts the capacity for love toward all God's creatures. Do not cease to put forth your best efforts and activity, and all else shall be added thereunto. We are the adventurers in fortune, you Sons of God on the earth plane, and we on the Spiritual. There can only be progress as we cooperate.

Do not allow Mind to intrude and wreck progress you may make as you proceed onward in interpreting these matters. Instead, shut Mind further and further away and lean harder and harder on Spirit. Your creative powers for any line of earthly work are strongest then, if you could but realize it. Too often you doubt in your subconscious minds that certain things are coming to pass, and you do what you call "worry" over them. There is no need for this worry, as it only blocks the very thing that it seeks to remedy. Overcome it by perfect trust in the Elder Brother of us all, and His disciples and servants over here.

IT HAS been many ages since the spirits that have since become known as Men arrived upon this earth-plane, engaged in creative mischief with the spirit particles developing here, and imbedded qualities into their composition that were never intended to disclose there. Time is no factor in such an operation. Time as you know it in your dimension does not exist in ours in quite the same fashion, or what might be called Degree of Appreciation. Time for the transpiration of events of a given character is one thing; time as an appreciation of transpiration of something in your minds is quite something else. It may be conditioned by your enjoyment of it, or your want of it, or your need of it. Time as Time is the same in all planes of conscious thought, of course. But it may pass swiftly when you are engaged in something beautiful or desirable, and drag interminably when you are engaged in something unpleasant or distasteful.

In the case of the regenerating spirits, it has gone swiftly enough, but not so swiftly that it has exhausted the remedies it first sought to achieve.

The adventuring spirits from distant planets came to earth because it appeared to be an extremely desirable place to learn their Lessons of Eternity, and gain to a knowledge of what it meant to minister to lesser forms of creation. They were not exactly vicious in what they conceived to be the occupancy of Thought-Forms for their own purposes. Those changes came gradually in their thought concepts. They saw what could be created by the powers of Thought and experimented to see how far their own experiences in manifested organisms could carry them. But soon they were plunging into sensuous enjoyments and naught else. Sensuous enjoyments occupied all their "thought time" to the exclusion of spiritual educatings. Sensuous enjoyments and naught else, was their shibboleth. They "forgot themselves", we might put it. They forgot who they were, and what they were, and for what creative and constructive purposes they had first sought out earth. You get the same thing today in the cases of those extremely self-centered people who care nothing for the rights or experiences of others but concentrate solely on having a good time, no matter what the cost to neighbors or relatives. "Thinking about others" appears foolish or infantile. Such people, after a little, concentrate strictly on their own thought-patterns, what they can do purely to prolong their own indulgences and enjoyments.

We tell you it is mischief, all of it. It was mischief when it started and it continues to be mischief, down here into the present. But let us tell you this—

Spirits who go in for this sort of thing have tough experiences coming to them, in pleasure-pain endurances. They go into a thing expecting pleasure, find it ending in pain, and bemoan the fact that life is unkind and the God of Creation "cruel".

There is no unkindness and there is no cruelty. As well blame God for being cruel when they thrust their fingers into the cogwheels of a machine and find the fingers can be crushed. By calling God cruel for giving them educating experiences, they are saying in effect that He should have provided them with fingers that did not crush when thrust into the cogwheels of machines ☼

Over long series of ages the spirits of men who were once higher than angels, have sunk lower than beasts in their own satisfactions, and mischievous self-indulgences. But they can—and will—eventually come back. That is the Plan of Salvation, we tell you solemnly. They will eventually all perceive the "unrighteousness" of following their own selfish desires and sensuous pursuits, and return to what originally was their "holy angelic status" . .

That means they will give serious attention to the business of being angelic as now they are prone to give serious attention to the business of being beastly.

You dear brethren who open your hearts to Light and keep them open, may have come so far already that you are almost graduated out of the beastly defilements in your essence, or you were among the Minions of Light who volunteered to accompany the Great Avatar and do what you could, life after life, in helping to restore the "perverted creation" back to what God Himself originally visualized it. If the latter—and only in your own bosoms is the true secret of identity locked—then do not bemoan the privilege of coming back age after age and life after life to make good on your original brevet and ministration. You are not consigned to a treadmill of endurance. You are allotted the privilege of helping the Christ and augmenting His success ✠ And that is too wonderful and marvelous to even discuss in your present purblindness of concept and envelope of earthly flesh. Just trust that it is truth and that the time will come when all of you who belong to the original Goodly Company will have it revealed to you in flashings of brightest radiance . .

The "Work of the Lord" is going forward, we repeat, and going higher and higher, generation by generation, and age by age. It is something to glory in . .

There is no reason why you Sons and Daughters of Radiance should ever be in trouble of any kind if you will only let your original Love Spirit guide you consciously in everything you attempt. It is the only real force in the world that truly accomplishes what you term Miracles, and brings you the things constructively that you seek. People you are not aware of, feel it, and act upon it in your behalf when they do not recognize the source of their cooperations. The whole fabric of society is becoming motivated by it, and absence of it brings complications of fret, misfortune and failure. You want to remember that as the Great Teacher extended His love to you, so you want to extend it to others, to bring out the best that is in them and help them fastest to get back to their lost angelic status so that the Work of the Lord may at last know completion. Your problems are really but one problem then—GIVE OF YOURSELVES AND YOU SHALL RECEIVE! You are commended to go forward to the work of your days in freedom and poise and love. When you feel pangs of doubt, think of the words we have been able to get through to your understandings by this route and instrument. The ways of God are NOT the ways of humanity, but you can make them so by obedience to His will. Thousands of you, even those of you who have spent endless ages here at the work of assisting the Elder Brother, do not fully trust even today His promise to provide for you.

We tell you He is in your hearts every moment, if you will but acknowledge His presence there. The trouble afflicting most of you lies in your subconscious minds, and you will not be able to "straighten yourselves out" till you give Him one hundred percent cooperation in your hearts. There is only one way to do this—
RELAX TO HIM ALTHOUGH BUSY TO THE WORLD!

BEAR WITH us while we develop this theme a bit further: We have said that you must learn first, last, and always, the real meaning of Love. Wisdom you must also know, for Love without Wisdom is a paradox ✡

Wisdom is the highest point to which humanity may aspire because it is the perfect synchronization between Love and Intelligence—hence between Soul and Spirit.
¶ When Love becomes sentimentality, or mere emotionalism, then it is Love divorced from Intelligence and therefore not Wisdom.

When the world uses the word Love, it means almost always the emotion that attends on Love, which may have no kinship whatever with the divine force. It is thus that we see the apparent impossibility of selfish love, or even foolish love, or too indulgent love. There can be no such thing. If Love is more than an emotion, it is wise with the instinctive wisdom inherent in the Great Creative Force in the Universe.

When Love is truly Love, it sees first and foremost and clearly the highest need of the beloved, and its whole effort is to minister to that need, utterly regardless of return or reward. There are few in the flesh who can so love, and fewer still who can love not only those whose destiny is linked with theirs but all the world.
Love is the Creative Force!
LOVE IS SPIRIT IN ACTION!
In the human equation, Love is the creator of all that is in harmony with Universal Spirit. Then when this equation is accomplished, Love is its perfect flower ❧ ¶ So is Love the beginning and end of Man the Microcosm, as of the universe the Macrocosm. So is Love the beginning and the end, and so there is one beginning and one end, and hence no beginning and no end.

LOVE IS harmony, as we have said. But do you know how complex and wonderful are the laws even of musical harmony? Do you know the part that mathematics must play in the composing and rendering of the most spiritual and ethereal music?
There is harmony, indeed, in the whole universe and its laws are no less accurately worked out than the laws of music. You need not, of course, learn mathematical formula. The only thing to remember is, that for a really intellectual grasp of such problems as that of the Fourth Dimension, you would need the mind of an astronomer or even a musical genius. Death itself is but

a passing through into this Fourth Dimension. You live in it then, and FEEL its meaning, without being able to convert it into words.

All these laws of Love by which the Spirit works in the universe and in the souls of men, are not our immediate concern. From time to time we can give you glimpses into their workings and into the Inner Meaning of the Fourth Dimension. But it will come out in connection with other matters and will be a feeling such as those on This Side have, rather than an intellectual realization. Now to return to Love—

Love must accomplish its end by the use of Harmony, but after your many visits to earth in pursuit of the brevet you have taken upon yourselves, you will have learned the mathematics of that Harmony and become able, so to speak, to compose by instinct.

So when your human soul is in its highest developed state it is able to operate in accordance with laws of Harmony it has no conscious knowledge of. But these intricacies ARE safely stored in Subconscious Memory. ¶ It is this which you mean when you say that you have recognized a "kindred spirit" . . you have become conscious of the synchronization of vibrations of whose very existence you were hitherto unaware.

Your task is to keep yourself so finely and exquisitely attuned that you may never be unaware of the beauty of the tone that comes from such synchronization.

We have heard you remark that it is rather a sort of

subconscious compatibility that you recognize between yourselves and others, for which vibrations are responsible. But that is not quite so. Compatibility usually implies an intellectual parity of some kind and you may have this sense of Oneness with a child, a genius, or a moron. This is the explanation of many strange friendships and marriages.

Love, as the world is accustomed to use the word, is synonymous with almost everything in the universe excepting Love. Weakness, sentimentality, possessiveness, selfishness—all these are hidden under the sacred name of Love. But there is one touchstone . .

If Love be truly present, you may know it by the miracles it works. Weakness becomes strength. Sentimentality becomes sympathy without pity. Possessiveness becomes the desire to serve. Selfishness becomes selflessness. And all of life flows together in one joyous rhythm until earth is lost in heaven and heaven is in man's heart.

When you are vibrating at a rate that raises you above the ordinary run of human vibration, you have the power to carry others with you to a higher point than they could get alone. Love and Harmony are the only creative forces—the ONLY forces in the creative sense of the word.

There is nothing to be solved in this problem but the question of technique. You have the spiritual light. The more often you succeed in bringing the light into consciousness by thought of Truth, the nearer you come to knowing the secret of control. When an author begins to write fiction that interests the multitude, he blunders technically. So when you first begin to regain your one-time angelic bodily control, you may blunder technically. And the same thing goes for emotional control, or control of thought that brings you back into a true appreciation of yourself, AND WHAT YOU HAVE BEEN BEFORE THESE PRESENT LIVES ☥ You must see that the first steps of physical care are taken, and then that responsibility is up to your minds.

BY ACKNOWLEDGING and being interested in these matters, and absorbing this doctrine which we have for you richly, you are identifying yourselves as spirits who are either winning out in their fight over the one-time beastly ingredient, as we have said, or spirits who came to this earth-planet originally to aid in the task of cosmic regeneration of your fellows. Try to keep this thought in mind. Whichever you are, you are a focal point for the spreading of light and knowledge for which the world suffers most in its present extremity. Coming into earth life again and again, we tell you, for the Sons of God is never any hardship . . it is more to be regarded as a privilege.

You have the privilege of serving; you have the privilege of enlightening. It is like being a bodily physician who thinks nothing of making calls on his patient again and again until the afflicted one's cure is complete ¶ Would a true physician bemoan the fact that he had to call upon his patient again and again, that he was unable to work a cure in the single visitation?

Get the thought of your earthly predicament out of your thinking and concentrate on the joys of remedying that and those who are afflicted and who need you ¶ What difference does it make WHERE you exist, if you exist in the happy knowledge that you are serving?
¶ We tell you there is no greater happiness. In fact, that IS happiness, and anything else is a form of sensuous enjoyment which you are striving in your fineness of spirit to surmount . .

Not all, of course, are aware of this necessity for earthly return, until they have progessed through the Planes of Thought awaiting them in the more intricate dimensions. Thousands of people arrive in the discarnate state daily believing they have attained to the heaven of Biblical allegory because they find themselves surrounded by peace and dignity and order, with the turmoils of earth ceasing to be of moment. But sooner or later they "miss something" . . it occurs to them that no conditions of assured bliss redound to them in their new environments, they are to all intents and purposes the people they have always been, and they wonder about it. Only after lengthy instruction and awakening of their cosmic memories on the Thought Planes, do they become convinced that earthly re-existence must be an important part of life, and they proceed around the Thought Cycle to arrive at the conclusion that reentry into physical conditions is not only desirable but necessary, if they are to achieve what they aspire to achieve for their souls' eternal profit.

Do not be troubled by this at present. We have much to say to you upon it that require days and weeks and perhaps months to make clear to you. Some parts of it, we tell you, even souls old in wisdom do not comprehend entirely. However, we will instruct you as we can. Not all persons "go around the Thought Cycle" in full awareness of where they are traveling. It is a process of Nature and they acquiesce to it. We beg you to have patience until you come to understand it . . .

THE ELDER BROTHER

THE ELDER BROTHER

I NOTICED, as I went along with this instruction, that two sets of mentors seemed to be addressing me—or rather, mentors and a Mentor. The Masters of the Wisdom, whoever they were, had graciously begun supplying me with information that helped me to awaken with all dispatch to the brevet they implied I had taken on myself, to enlighten the wayward sons of men in this generation in the mysteries of their earthly predicament. Then from time to time, the Great Mentor—if we may call Him such—stepped in, and went further than they did, or rather, emphasized the more basic matters. I wasn't particularly interested, as these Sages should have known, in a mere program of "sweetness and light" that affected to solve all the problems of the universe in ten easy lessons of what is called Thought Control. In the first place, I never believed anyone could solve the problems of the universe in a hundred thousand lessons of Thought Control, no matter who sponsored them. What I wanted was hard practical enlightenment on how all of us got in this worldly mess, and what the big majority of us should do to attempt to pull out of it.

The Sages who came to me at first seemed to be beautiful souls, and wise souls, who were fairly familiar with the accepted fundamentals of metaphysics. Certainly nothing they had to tell me did me any damage. But when the Elder Brother came into the picture and began "vibrating" over the Pencil, He seemed to take me several steps deeper, down under the wisdom, and have things to disclose that the "sweetness and light" Sages elected to ignore. Little reference was made, I realized, in the delineations of the Sages, to the original sodomic perversion that raised such mischief with the human species in antediluvian days. The Elder Brother appeared to refer to it constantly.

So I had two sets of revelations, I might call it—the revelations vouchsafed me by the Sages, and the revelations vouchsafed me by the Master Teacher. Of the two, I preferred the Master Teacher's, not because He was the Master Teacher but because His references and disclosures seemed to make the better sense.

One couldn't be a normal man, of reasonably astute intellect in the twentieth century, and not observe that something fundamentally rotten afflicted the human race. Some people were "naturally" angelic, it seemed, and others were besotted beasts and workers of iniquities for the sheer love of the turmoil they stirred up. There had to be, I observed to myself, some adequate and rational reason for these two sets of people in a world where natural conditions had treated both classes more or less alike.

People didn't become angelic out of hand, I argued to myself. Neither were other men brutish and vicious out of hand, regardless of the iniquities of their ancestors. I had done much thinking about it. So when the Master Teacher came to me with this sodomic explanation for the swinish quality in an exceedingly large proportion of the so-called human race, He had a willing listener.

I was puzzled of course, by many unexplained things. I didn't have it expounded to my satisfaction who God was, or what the Godhead was, or who the Master Teacher meant when He referred constantly to "the Father" . . seeing that the Sages had first instructed me that there was no God aside from Holy Spirit. But that there might have been an influx of interstellar spirits into this earth-scheme, who raised mischief with the forms of developing biologic life they found here, was reasonable enough explanation for the brutishness in some people so that I was willing to await clarification of the mystery—and, please heaven, it did come to me in time. However—

The Master Teacher seemed agreeable to disclosing things to me which the Sages fought shy of, and if in these reprinted papers there seems to be a discrepancy here and there between the preachments of the Sages and the enlightenments of the Master Teacher, I adjure my reader to attribute explanation to this difference in authorship. I can truthfully assure my said reader that after twenty years of instruction, the confusion came clear to me, and in the proper place I shall treat with it. There was something authentic about the disclosures of the Master Teacher, however, that kept me eternally taking messages. His Personality began to seem familiar to me. I waited for His presence and always had the adequate wisdom delivered across the Pencil.

And why did it come to me? I choose to think it was because I conceded some long-buried obligation on my part to release this intelligence to present-day mankind —to give my whole career to it, even at the sacrifice of my worldly achievements to the moment.

NE THING I can truthfully say: I began to get a new and perturbing envisionment of this Elder Brother—an estimate of His personality and psychology that I found in no scriptural passages. He was someone I seemed to have known intimately in a long-buried incarnation, and what He had to transfer to me was merely a modern reiteration of something ancient, entombed in my subconscious.

People, I gradually came to accept, did not vacate their bodies at physical death and waft themselves off to some mythical heaven of golden streets and crystal fountains; they stayed right here in their old haunts and scenes, in contact with those they loved and who loved them, until the time came for a general exodus of all in a given family or class or group into higher regions of radiance.

This checked with what we seemed to be learning from the more advanced findings of psychical science. In that Higher Dimension of Consciousness, the Lord of Calvary still had His transcendent Being, and still watched and guided and counselled the world in its complicated modern problems. In, or from, that Higher Dimension, I was conceited enough to accept that He was enabled to address His thoughts to me with no less difficulty than He had addressed His rebuke to Saul of Tarsus: "Saul, Saul, why persecutest thou Me?" The fact that the last had been done in the first century and the speech to me addressed in the twentieth, was a mere detail. Time meant nothing in the Dimension in which He existed. And why wasn't I just as consequential a human being as Saul? Who was Saul, that he should be venerated especially because the phenomenon had happened to him in the first century instead of the twentieth? I refused to back down to him. I never had liked his personality, anyhow.

Certainly if Jane, the grocer's daughter, could preserve her personality, so as to return in a psychical clinic and discuss the doings in the grocer's family with her surviving relatives, so greatly an advanced personality as the Teacher of Galilee should be able to do the same, when He was in contact with someone who could rebroadcast His intelligence to a million souls—as I was able to do from my position as national author and publisher. I don't think it was altogether conceit on my part. It was recognition of what I represented as a practical channel for passing along His adjurations to the current human race.

What He seemed to imply, about my having been with Him in Galilee, could be left to the future Thought-State to determine. Maybe I had been, maybe I hadn't. I didn't recognize that it made any difference. If I was in touch with the Master Brain of all ages, and was willing and even eager to disseminate what He had to say to the bedeviled human race of the present, that was that. Why shouldn't it be me as well as the next man?

After all, it was the intelligence, not the question of personal vanities, that counted.

Was it any more phenomenal for me to meet and talk with the Elder Brother while on this plane than a couple of hours after my heart had ceased beating?

I certainly expected to do that!

As the more Intimate Teacher, and Advanced Mentor, He referred constantly to the mischief done the man-species back in the sodomic era and apparently predicated the whole scheme of salvation on the one-time diabolism of it. If He wanted corrective instruction distributed throughout the world today, I was willing to distribute it. I came to the place where, for weal or woe, I cast my whole writing career aside and went into the business of circulating this subliminal information among my distraught fellowmen.

HE GREAT Teacher seems to attach the utmost stress to the abominations of the sodomic period, I say, more than the "sweetness and light" Sages who opened this enlightenment to me, and who even today continue to supply it. He seems to believe that the human race IS making progress up from its original bestiality, into the great clear radiance of the true eternal verities. And so long as He is satisfied with what is being achieved, I can only follow His lead and accept it myself. After all, He is judge.

Now where is the end of it all to find us, and is there an end? The point is important.

On the 1st day of March, 1929, I found myself transcribing a communication that is entitled in my manuscript books, "If I But Gave the Word!" and I think it belongs in this volume for light that it supplies on the vast cosmic drama which we are actors in today, or which is being played out, at least, before our eyes. I shall have more to say about the Great Teacher in future chapters, not only in this book but in other volumes which are coming. This Man of Galilee, about whom there are more books being written, and more text being penned, 1950 years after His birth than at any other time in the world's history, seems to be the arbiter of this planet in ways which the ordinary run of humankind little realizes.

Let me reprint this fateful Master Communication of His, in the next few pages, and see if it leaves the awesome impression upon you that it left upon me, that night twenty years or more bygone when I made it of sacred record . .

THE REVELATION

If I But Gave the Word!

MY DEARLY BELOVED:

WE GATHER as agreed; the day is well spent; the night findeth us with labors performed. Now, My dear ones, let Me make lengthy speech with you. Ye have come far with Me; I have come farther with you. We have conversed together over many details of policy. Now I make known to you how we proceed further and more effectively.

Know that I so loved the world that I gave it My life. My life was the price paid for man's possession.

Man was doomed to extinction—as man—many ages ago. His thoughts were of darkness. He loved the darkness. His animal perversions had blotted his divinity. The Plan had not been successful for him as a creation of method and order. He had despoiled his own house. The evil which he had done was abomination. He had made antics of the Father's beneficence; he had made riot in holy places; his whole creation was a misanthropy.

Know that I did pity him for his dumbness and impatience. Know that I gave up residence on Higher and Farther Planes to be close to material earth and try to bring order from his chaos.

Know that I so loved suffering humankind that I did enter into a compact: I OFFERED THE FATHER MY LIFE IN EXCHANGE FOR THE LIVES OF THE WORLD . .
My life was not desired of the Father but He was so touched by my sacrifice of higher and greater and vaster joys of eternities that He gave Me the earth-plane upon a condition:
I was to come into the world as an humble Unknown. I was to live as one of those whose wickedness of ordeal was an abomination. I was to know Pain and Suffering and Physical Death, but I was likewise to know Resurrection for a purpose . .
The world might thereby take to heart the example of My life and have before it an ideal of permanent divinity ⚚

I CAME INTO the world to save it from physical, literal extinction. There would have been a heavenly holocaust. Stars would have fused. Mankind would have perished as a created order. There would have been no world as men now know the world.
They were not to know that I had bought them thus for the price of an ideal. They were to think Me human. They were to be shown what human creation could accomplish ⚚
I gave them example until my thirtieth year.
Then came the Father's angels to Me. We did sit upon

a mountain-top and discuss mankind. I did come down from that mountain with the determination strong within me to save humankind even at the cost of physical death, hoping to show man thereby that even death of the body can be conquered by Faith.

So they killed Me. They did spit upon Me and revile Me. They did make mock of heaven and orderly love.
¶ Well knew I that they might do such things. Well knew I that I was as sheep among wolves. Well knew I that I had volunteered for a mission of ignominy that I might hoist a petard of hope before the ranks of the doomed ☩

Apprise ye the sad result . .

I CAME into this world and it received Me not. I did open the eyes of those who were blind and lo they saw not. Gave I the water of life to the perishing and they did make sport of that, my generosity. The Beast lingered in them. They stayed unclean. Yet did I persevere for I knew there was a spark of Great Divinity in the hearts of bestial men and I would save it!

I knew that sooner or later men might come to see that the order of creation might be brought back to the Father, whom I served as Son.

Waxed I industrious in My ministrations. Gave I freely of time and effort and persevering compassion though they stoned Me and reviled Me and made mock of Me.

Yet did I triumph over death and come back as Witness of the lost idealism.

The world was slow to acknowledge Me, yet acknowledge Me it did. In that acknowledgment were the hands of My devoted disciples—the people of the Goodly Company—who returned with Me to earth again and again, times beyond counting, seeking to turn men's hearts and faces in the Upward Way.

Yea, and even ye were on earth time and time again. Yea, did ye work and preach and expound and reveal. Yea, did ye die even as I died, that men might know the love I brought them from far, far planes. Yea, and did ye preach Me in a score of guises, generation upon generation, until ye be yourselves of the present, seeking in My world to turn men's hearts to the Higher Way. Verily I honor you for such service.

Now do ye not see why we come ear to ear in the flesh? The world maketh progress toward the Father, yet is it ever retarded by the sons of darkness. They are workers of iniquity in that they love iniquity. The Beast hath left its mark upon them. Generation unto generation it showeth its fangs.

They who have been of good report have suffered cruelly because of those who clung to the darkness. They who grew to love Me and keep My commandments of loving service, were reviled and slain by the workers of iniquity.

Sorely, sorely, hath My patience been tried. Sorely

have I doubted if My work and sacrifice were of merit and worthy of the time and pain. Sorely have I been tempted to let the holocaust appear and go unto My Father in the apex of Spirit Creation and there abide. Yet ever have I been touched by the sight of the cowering, they who would walk uprightly if they but had no fear. Ever have I beheld the humble lift up their hands for enlightenment.

These have made Me rejoice. These have caused Me to be of faith that down far generations the world might be entirely cleansed of the Mark of the Beast.

So ever was it thus. So it will be. So is the errand and the mercy thereof.

Man hath shown willingness unto redemption. He hath shown less and less of the brute in his heart. Verily hath he made progress up from the darkness, and I say unto you it augureth well. Still have we seen the Beast stalking, however. With the angelic in man it conflicteth continually.

TODAY have I been with Thought Incarnate, the Principle of Created Matter. There I communed with the Spirit of the Ghost. There have I seen mysteries too great for mortal mind to grasp. There were ye once, My greatly beloved, but ye do have brains of earth intervening in the exposition thereof.

I tell you I have given account to the Ghost of the work I have done upon this planet. The Word is:

Well done, Beloved, continue Thou in grace. So we meet back upon the plane of earthly thought tonight. The world little suspecteth how slender is the thread on which hangeth its perpetuation.
IF I BUT GAVE THE WORD, lo the heavens would shower fire, the continents would tremble, and the night of inky blackness would fall upon the cinder of a Once-World that would fuse with other nomad planets and form a flashing nebula far into empty heavens.
BUT I GIVE NOT SUCH WORD!
I keep within the hollow of My pierced hand the safety of this planet. I tend and watch it.
Daily I see the life of nations. I watch pranking statesmen make mock of our labors over many generations and I rebuke them not, knowing that if there be but a spark of the Holy Ghost within them, it will one day redeem them.
I watch the humble rise to affluence and give good accounting of their talents, and am encouraged. So be it. Now come I to things of lesser tenor—

WE ARE of one substance. We are of one flesh to save the humbler seekers after Truth from the Mark of the Beast. We come to save the humble and the worthy, and take them up to the Father. Our work goeth on in progressive stages. One by one do we eliminate great social cancers. One by one do we despoil the idols of Mammon and tear apart the altars of

connivance for nefarious ends. One by one do we eliminate the princes of evil from their petty thrones, setting up potentates under us who are of the Goodly Company. Now mark this, beloved—
I AM COMING BACK TO THE EARTH-PLANE IN PERSON! I have said this before; I say it again.
Sufficient do I consider the numbers of the progressing ones to encourage them by a demonstration of miraculous power and personal appearance. They will hear of My living presence and leap joyously.
Others who are doomed to the Great Extinction will be angered and vindictive and revengeful and murderous, crying: What have we to do with Thee, Thou Son of Light?
I come in time of great world tumult when the powers of earth arrange themselves for murder in rows. I come to visit My righteous wrath on those who mark My Goodly Company for their slaughtering. I come to blast them with My scorn and wither them with My righteous indignation. Let us consider the result . . Great nations are not led of great statesmen, I tell you.
They do the behest of the widely advertised, not the truly great in heart. They do follow demagogues who rant of war when war threateneth, and rant of peace when peace is popular. They are worldly sheep led of blind shepherds who do consort with wolves.
Ye are of patient endurance, My beloved. I speak for your high instruction. Nations are led of demagogues,

I tell you, whose politicians have but selfish ends to serve. They are not of real international mind; they care not for real human brotherhood; ever they seek after self-exploitation. No spirituality have they to perceive the real causes behind world tumult. They live only for the rewards of clamor and the plaudits of reward. They do seek to perform the opportune, not that which is permanently just, in their councils of state. I tell you this, beloved, as your background.

Fear not any statesman who seeketh only his own reward of merit—he is as a hollow reed through which the wind bloweth. I say unto you, your task is to winnow the mongers of hate from the shepherds of eternal peace and light. Your task it is, to walk in Light and await the Great Speaking. Your task it is, to show yourselves unto those who are bedeviled and by speech that I will put in your lips, make the earth's vain potentates to realize that My beloved are among them again, steadfastly working as of old—the cornerstone of My presence on earth, of which I once spoke. Your task it is, to speak unto men as I shall direct you, making them to understand that a Great Miracle soon cometh.

Tell them not of the Miracle's nature but deal mystically, as one who knoweth the secret of a living world and yet abideth in wise silence until the speaking of it worketh good.

Take heart, beloved. Be of bright countenance. This day have I borne witness of you in worlds ye know not

of. This day have I communed with the Spirit Behind All Creation and heard the pronouncement: So be it! The world is redeemed, I tell you, by the sacrifice of your spirit and compassionate administration.
Blessed be your names!
Spirit Divine am I, Spirit divine are ye. Spirit divine we manifest in flesh. Spirits Ennobled do we go before the Host and give accounting of our trust. Lo, the world is made to see the Father's works manifest in us, and we shall be its saviors.

BELOVED, rejoice! Tonight I rejoice! Be known of Me! Know that great events impend. Great wars are on their way. Great murders will be attempted. We stand adamant, saying unto the Beast: Get hence! Be gone! Leave the sheepfold of humanity and let the upright know their shepherds.
Unto you, My beloved, a mission cometh. We are of splendorful cooperation. We are of easier access as the days ensue. We know in our hearts that we have love for the world, but we know not who in the world may love us until they manifest that love.
Harken, beloved! Wait and study and write and watch! Take note of the godlike; give heed to the pious. Be of compassion for the earnest in human endeavor, no matter what their creed or race or religious persuasion. Do you know them as brothers. Go ye to and fro in the earth and up and down in it. Be of observng eye. Take

note of council halls. Be intimate with publicists who write of vast affairs. Many, I tell you, I will turn into your pathways.

Go ye to and fro with ministers of state. Sit at their boards. Talk with them privately. Know ye the world as the rooms of your dwelling-house.

Go to and fro constantly, I tell you. When ye have learned a tongue, pass on. Go east, go west. Commune with Me ever daily. See great scenes, watch vast spectacles, know ye no resting-place excepting the home to which ye do come at intervals with these, your devoted companions. Travel far, I say. Let no man know of your comings or your goings. The day approacheth down years of important developings when ye shall be wiser than all earthly potentates. Great shall be your voices for the acquaintings which ye have. Then shall the governments of earth seek counsel of the Goodly Company and in the Morn of the Great Speaking, ye My beloved, shall stand forth for whom ye are!

MY BELOVED, I charge you: be of good report. Always remember that ye are My disciples who have not tasted of death until I shall have come again. Ye are My brethren, My children, and My friends. We are workers together upon planes of Love. We go to and fro, forever doing good. The good which we do sheweth the Goodly Company that we are its leaders and shepherds and augurers.

This night have I spoken unto you privately. I have told you the secret of the world's predicament. Go far and move constantly, I tell you, knowing no rest until I bid you rest. Seek Me and Mine, north, south, west and east. Prepare yourselves, beloved, to stand before kings in the wisdoms of earth. Know tongues. Know manners and customs and brevets of courts. Seek ye worldly experiences with Godlike reserve. Be of circumspect speech and yet open of ear. Know that ye do gather information that ye may be shepherds of the Goodly Company, in and after the Day of the Miracle. I speak whereof I know.

Think well of the future—I arrange it. Changes come, as the Beast seemeth to strengthen or to weaken, but your communication is the same to the end.

The work of Holy Spirit is the work of eternity. We do it joyously. Peace and a wondrous union to you when the brevet is ended and the work is closed!

This is My communication unto you tonight. We are workers in the worlds, seeking mankind's eternal profit. The Sons of Darkness must have their little day obstructing us. Thus it is written. They do hasten to and fro, casting barriers in our pathways.

I say, let them do it. Presently cometh a conviction unto them that earthly life satisfieth them not. They are cast down in their imaginings. The Host visiteth them not. They are of vain conceits. They know not where to hide their heads.

We are compassionate towards them in that day and guide them back into the pathways of the Father. I say unto you, do it!
Thus do we complete a brevet begun long ago in the Father's eternal councils. We are laborers in the worlds for mankind's endless profit . .

THE GOODLY COMPANY

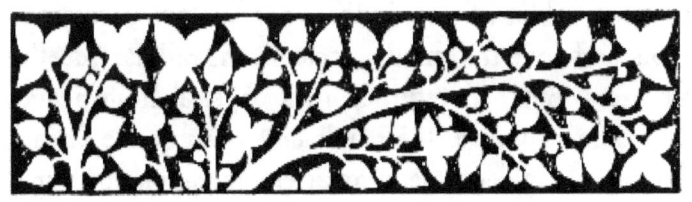

THE GOODLY COMPANY

IF YOU were a person of certain literary attainments, who had lived a reasonably normal and successful life to the moment, never suspecting that any such awesome or consequential brevet awaited you, and suddenly had such an extraordinary communication addressed to you by a phenomenal means, would you set it down to the vaporings of subconscious mind or would you not? Delusions of grandeur? Such things had happened. But what a peculiar aspect of delusions of grandeur! There was in the world, apparently, a coterie of persons who might well be designated as the reborn souls of the patriarchs and martyrs of old, who had never gone through the full experiences of dy-

ing since Biblical times, in that they had never entered upon, and gone the lengthy cycle of, the ordinary death processes, but had returned into physical flesh again and again to uphold the hands and work of the Great Teacher of Galilee generation after generation down into the present, and if the text could be credited, I had something to do with them—and was expected to have considerable more to do with them.

What did it gain me to doubt or question it?

Nothing vicious nor mischievous was being proposed in the text. It stated irrevocably that goodly works were in progress in the earth, that mankind was gradually working out a vast spiritual redemption within itself, that there were principals incarnated in flesh who were supposed to advance and speed up that work—to the honor and glory of the Great Avatar who sponsored it. Even if subconscious mind and delusions of grandeur were responsible for what had been recorded, the end was meritorious which the brevet described.

However, there were occasional phenomena in connection with such transcriptions, the nature of which I can't divulge upon this page. How account for those?

I did the obvious and human thing. I took the text as bona fide and governed my thinking and life and career accordingly. And more and more expositions of wisdom continued to arrive for me. Strange doors began opening to me. Stranger people began to introduce themselves to me as though by a sort of mundane appointment. Some of them, I discovered, HAD SIMILAR COMMUNICATIONS IN THEIR FILES—similar in context if not in diction. In the ensuing two years after I had started to release in printed form the intelligence I had received, 20,000 people people flocked to me and around me to obtain all such "wisdom" I possessed to release to them.

The Goodly Company? What else could I think? The evidence was coming to my attention independent of my own activities.

Why did I go off upon a political departure that seemed for a time to delay in ignominy? Because it was part of my instruction that I should do what I did. If the very essence of the sodomic beast lingering in man is not apparent in those "rulers" who dictate the destinies of Soviet Russia, then where should I expect to apprehend them? Was it not beasthood and darkness at its worst? I chose to think so, and still choose to think so. Common sense told me that Communism was the Beast at its strongest.

At the time of transcribing the foregoing message, take note, World War II was a decade in the future. As of this writing—May 20, 1950—World War III is still ahead of all of us. "Great wars are on their way" the message had stated in 1929—and note that "wars" is used in the plural. We live in an era when the Piscean Age—or celestial month—is closing, and the Aquarian Age opening. Such periods are attended by vast social disturbances. We are knowing them at present and must perceive them for what they are. There are other communications in my files, I tell you, that describe the time and method of this Second Coming in smallest detail. Subconscious mind? What IS subconscious mind? How do we know that prenatal memory may not contribute to much that is stored in the subconscious?

I am making no claims to anything supernatural—I am narrating to you what happened . .

HE IMPORTANT point is, there seem to be three classes, or castes, of mortal life on earth today: the indigenous forms that we might designate as the product of biologic evolution; the Sons of God who arrived via a great migration through interstellar space and who "looked upon the daughters of earth and saw that they were fair and chose of them wives" who produced the progeny of the appalling sodomic period; and the members of the Goodly Company—estimated from other sources to be around 144,000—who followed here with the Great Avatar and have been promoting His work of redemption for nameless thousands of years. Here are these three forms, or castes of life, "all mixed up" apparently, or at least getting themselves born and living after the flesh, pursuing conventional careers of ordinary mortal people, but putting what qualifying

spiritual enhancements into life that they can by example and precept, and generally supplying humankind with a high spiritual standard by which to live. And the only way that one can be discerned from the other is by the nature and quality of their characters as demonstrated in their works!

Assuredly it does account for the grievously "mixed up" classes of society that we find deploying around the world today . .

Of thirty persons in a given street-crowd, ten may be the beast-progeny of the ape-mothers of long ago, ten may be reincarnated spirits from the original Sirian migration, and ten may be members of the Goodly Company of the Avatar, trying to repair the moral damage done so long ago when the members of the Migration ran riot in sodomy—and yet all thirty appear the same as to physical members and, viewed externally, show only differences of racial features and dress. The only way by which they may be identified is by observing their spiritual manners and employments. Multiply that given street-crowd by millions—and even billions —and you have the worldly situation with its conflict of temperaments that makes society what it is, and human progress what it isn't!

Making the concept of it the backlog of one's thinking, nevertheless, does lead to other explanations for both cosmic and mundane mysteries that commence to put sense into the whole worldly picture.

The people of the whole world, apparently, are working out a gigantic laboratory experiment in spiritual eugenics. Infiltrated through all ranks and classes of society are the persons identified as the Avatar's Aides, living normal lives themselves, attracting no attention to their advanced spiritual status except by demonstrations of the Christlike qualities that are second nature to them, and constituting a perpetual exhibit of what the whole world should be, to have everlasting peace and righteousness among men. They are, as Christ said constantly during His Galilean ministry, the little yeast that leavens the whole loaf.

Thus the earthly drama is being played out.

The "beasts" still incarnate and perpetuate their beastliness, hating the Avatar and the Avatar people, and all the latter's works. The "beasts" want to be let alone to dominate the planet and do as they please. They lose no opportunity to disparage and smear and imprison and kill anyone whose outstanding endeavors mark them unmistakably as one of the Christus Assistants. Even when they have their own way at times, it brings them no lasting satisfaction—as they frequently concede. Still, dominating is one of their major obsessions. And the Avatar Aides must suffer from their antics. It is an entirely new slant on this vast sodomic picture of world conflicts and confusions.

Popular psychology contends that the differences in humankind come from hereditary and environmental ingredients. Yet popular psychology offers no solution for the curiosity that two people, stood side by side, and put through identical experiences, will come from those experiences with as much spiritual profit on the one side as there is injury or loss on the other. Modern biology offers the infusion of different varieties of genes as accounting for the classifications of human temperament derived from hereditary factors. It does not account for physically enhoused souls being different in their essences, because one man's eyes are blue and another man's brown, or because one woman is a blonde and another a brunette. It is all an attempt—biology is —to predicate the spiritual on the physically organic. What most of us want to know is, why are some people naturally and inherently vicious and others naturally and inherently altruistic—and constructive and compassionate and long suffering and generous?

How happened it, when we come right down to considering it, that millions of years before there was any human intelligence observing occurrencs on this planet, cells were building up of themselves—apparently—into perfect aspects of organic functioning? The organic nsemble of the antediluvian dinosaurus was quite as intricate and facile in fuctioning as anything displaying in living form at present, and yet at the same time the creature had a brain so small that it could be put in an egg cup. Did there not have to be a Directing Intelligence to produce the organism of the dinosaurus millions of years before true man appeared on this planet, quite as well as the need for Directing Intelligence in forming man's ape-body of today? How dare we maintain that the doughty organism of the dinosaurus came about by "chance" but that modern man is the product of uncanny creative sagacity? What uncanny creative sagacity, and when, and under what conditions, did it begin to perform?

Y CURIOSITY about these deeper matters became so insatiable that all of mid-1929 was given over to seeking clairaudient information, particularly about the membership of the Goodly Company, and on the night of September 29, 1929, almost a year after I had done the original writing with Mary in New York, I received a dissertation on the subject of the "Christ Force'" that seemed to shed some more light on the creation and composition of other forms of life higher than the human.

A most peculiar woman had introduced herself into my affairs in New York. For purposes of identification I shall name her merely as Hazel. She was, I found to my astonishment, fifty-two years old, and yet she possessed the body and youthful charm of a girl of twenty-five. One feature about her remains outstanding in my memory—her uncanny eyes. She had the eyes of one of those celestial beings in a medieval painting—

unearthly eyes—the eys of a Madonna one moment and an entity "out of this world" the next. And her psychical and esoteric "gifts" wer so profound that at times they frightened me. Was she a human woman, I seriously asked myself? I had reason to question it. She had been born in Ohio back in the Eighties, lived a reasonably normal life but never married. At the time I came into contact with her she was holding down a high-salaried position with one of the biggest chemical companies in the east, obtaining formula for it psychically from which it was making millions. When she entered my apartment and sat herself down, she had only to go quiescent for me to find myself possessed of psychical motive power to accomplish all sorts of phenomenal venturings in my own right. Lastly, she had a disposition and temperament that could only be ascribed to an angel from heaven. And I wondered if she were that? I asked my mentors about her.

Well, I got the succeeding paper that introduced me to more elucidations about Higher Beings in this world. Looking back upon it from a twenty-year retrospect, I deem it appropriate to include that paper here in this volume on Guests from Other Planets . . .

There are not only the three classes of spiritual beings I have enumerated, here in earthly life, it seems; there are celestial messengers and "special agents" abroad in cosmos, who apparently incarnate now and then for particular purposes in either male or female bodies, depending on temperaments. Humanity long ago coined the word "angels" to describe these spirits. And I had evidently come upon one of them.

One of the most uncanny things I noticed about Hazel was her ability to find her way about an unlighted room as though it were fully illumined. I asked her about it once when I saw her go into a dark room and pick an object off a table.

"I've never known what other people call 'darkness'," she said, "in my life. Everything is in half-light. I was six or eight years old before I realized that others about me couldn't see as I could."

It didn't seem to occur to her that her order of creation had anything phenomenal about it. She accepted herself for what she was—precisely as the average person accepts his own humanness.

This is what the mentors had to say about her—

The Christ Force

HAZEL has had many incarnations that were all of one tenor, a ministering tenor. That is the essence of her being. Her incarnations have been peculiar, in that they have usually covered some specific work in the interests of the Christ Aides. They were started in the first place by your volunteering to come into life to interpret the Master without suitable equipment of your own to combat evil forces that would take advantage of your psychical blindness and impotency. You had work to do that was divine in its essence and therefore regulated by forces that have society in charge.

Now listen while we impart to you something not generally known or credited by the average run of humankind—

The agents of these forces are invariably the Beings whom you describe as Angels. We say "invariably" because they constitute a special order of creation higher than man constitutes, and organized to render specific service. Sometimes this service is fleshly, somtimes it is purely spiritual. It can be either.

You came into life countless centuries ago, at the behest of forces operating as the Christ Force, to do an interpretative work for the mortal race. This Christ

Force, of which you are a force, is complemented by the so-called angelic Host. This Host is an augmentation of the Christ Force in action. It constitutes a force that is frequently misnamed Holy Spirit. This Christ Force, of which Jesus of Nazareth was the living embodiment of its last manifestation, is the Life Force emanating from the Godhead and surcharging society with its ennoblements. This Force has other powers that manifest in Nature as elementals—which you do not understand. To get back, however, to angelic orders—

THERE are all sorts and castes and orders of Angels, as there are mortal beings. Some are One-Idea creatures, composed of living light, who only serve as messengers of Godhead pronouncements. Some there are who bring readings to humankind from other planets, telling it when and how to advance scientifically. Some are endowed with qualities of great persistence of office, who act as guards and watchers over those anointed by Holy Spirit—of whom Christ knew in the Garden when He referred to the "legions of angels" He could call up if He chose, to save Him the torture and ignominy of the cross ✞

But at the apex of them all stands a special coterie of beings whom we might best describe as Super-Angels, or those of such extraordinary capacity spiritually that they can manifest in any form desired for the accomplishment of their purposes.

Satan, or Lucifer as his name now is among men, was one of these, and well known is the story of how he used his transcendent powers wrongly. He is still in existence as an entity, we tell you, but shorn of many of his destructive capacities. He is not loose promiscuously, as so many theologians believe and teach, but is gradually being bound tighter and tighter by the Christ Forces, SO THAT HE IS RETROGRADING GRADUALLY INTO NONENTITY!

SUPER-ANGELS may be either male or female in their temperaments—for that is the only way that sex is determined Over Here—and may manifest in flesh as either men or women, but their errands on earth as either male or female have as their essence the aiding of the mortal mentors in recognizing their own identities and commissions.

We would say that in Hazel's case, she comes of a certain angelic order, accounting for many of her unearthly capabilities, and has been subconsciously aware of it over many generations. She has been made aware of it in other instances, you would find, which she has not revealed to you as yet—not that she is hiding it particularly, but the facts will be recognized as significant when revealed by Memory.

You have other such ministers and mentors around you whom we hesitate to speak of—we want you to find them out as you suspect you have found out Hazel . .

Great is the mission on which all of you Christ People have embarked, so great that only leading entities in man's present culture are in contact with you, supporting you, loving you, working in rapport with you. That goes for workers on This Side as well as on yours. Hazel is an entity of no mean character, the feminine prototype of Michaelena. Call it Sister in a manner of speaking, although it is a matter of temperaments as we have said.

Angels are sexless more than mortal, since they have no propensity for self-propagation in the physical sense. They can get themselves born of earthly parents in any instance they elect. Each one spiritually is specifically created by the Godhead, not coming from the ocean of spirit as men came, or even as the people of the migration or the Avatar's Aides came. Further elucidation of this will be supplied you later, a very deep mystery, unknowable as yet, until you have gone deeper into esoteric instruction for which at present you are not ripe. That they have "wings" of medieval representation is of course symbolic. Moving and functioning with the speed of light, they are symbolically presented as having wings, but factually that is fantastic. They can go and come as Thought goes and comes, and perform Thought's functions. Thus are they presented as being winged. Anatomically, wings upon a human being's physical person would be an anomaly . .

What we are trying to tell you is: Angels of themselves have no sex at any time, but may incarnate in physical bodies of apparently normal men and women for a purpose according to their temperaments. It would be very difficult for angels of masculine temperament to incarnate as mortal women—quite as difficult as for mortal women to incarnate as angels. On the other hand, a feminine angelic temperament would never incarnate in a man's body without revealing traits that would be offensive to both sexes.

Now what we have said amounts to this: You Christ People have a work to accomplish that requires the assistance of a large number of tremendous personalities to accomplish it. There are other angelic administrators coming into your lives whom you know not of, as yet. They will make themselves known to you as celestial entities by the services they render you. Do not be precipitous about discovering them.

The Goodly Company is an ensemble of perfected Master Spirits who volunteered once long ago to achieve a special mission. They were to incarnate over and over as normal men and women in every age, and among every race, and in every clime, but when the Christ Doctrine appeared and reappeared, they were to give it their support locally wherever they resided and thus infiltrate it among the common ranks of humankind until it became universally accredited.

Thus is progress effected throughout all society.

This is the mission they are performing today!

The Christ Spirit is ever-present to them. They are constantly and forever aware of the Christ's integrity and splendorful personality aiding and guiding and abetting them. There is no disposition on the part of the Christ Forces to come unto men and yet not come unto them—to acclaim themselves for that which they are and yet do nothing to affect it positively. They are the embodiment of all which is right and splendorful for the human race to achieve. They come and go in flesh at the command of Forces higher and more majestic than themselves and yet in humble capacities as well as great and significant capacities. They are ever present in society, bringing it back to its one-time-abandoned spiritual heritage . .

Do you acclaim yourselves as of that wondrous company if sobeit you feel the impulses of the Christ Personality bestirring in your breasts. It is the identification of your Divinity. No one is excluded as belonging to that Company, if he but feel its impulse.

The Work of the Lord goes forward in this generation with as assured a stride as it ever went forward in Palistine twenty centuries in the past. It is the Plan of Salvation that every last one shall be saved. None are cast out. None are ignored. Unto the microscopically least of all created human creatures the order of ultimate salvation comes.

GRASPING THE INFINITE

GRASPING THE INFINITE

EARN for a more peaceable and equitable world as they may, there comes a period in the lives of practically one hundred percent of people when a feeling of futility that amounts to despair assails them, that their lives are so inconsequential—when considered against the background of the two billion other persons populating the earth—and their histories and concerns so trivial as compared to the mass activities of races by epochs. The existence of the individual human unit is so brief, and its area of activity in any one life so restricted, that difficulty arises in conceiving that any one person is of importance outside his immediate circle of family and friends. That great Cosmos

should keep track of him in particular, or that what he does and how he lives his life should be of much concern in the summing-up of eternal progressions generally, is something he accepts in a sort of blind and desperate hope. Gray's "Elegy in a Country Churchyard" epitomizes the sentiment that more often fits the mood of these persons when they regard the myriad swarms of human beings that overrun the earth, living and working and marrying and dying year upon year and generation upon generation. And yet deep within the human spirit is an ineradicable hunger to be considered of importance, and an implacable thirst to do more drinking of the vitalities of life than the individual gnat in the swarm that rises and falls in the country air of summer sunset. Probably it was Christ's regard for the dignity and importance of the individual human person, and His sympathy and regard for the eternality of the individual as an individual that brought Him such acclaim and allegiance as the Son of God up across the generations since His death.

There is, in the human soul, a remonstrance against being considered a stereotyped nonentity that must have some greater and surer basis than merely a desire to partake of the dramas and vicissitudes of consciousness endlessly. The average human life, with its insufferable roster of aches and pains and frets and tragedies, is such a repellent experience at best, that it seems incomprehensible for people of any sense to want to enter it or prolong it—yet we know that they do, and struggle madly to preserve it. This is paradox at its best.

Over and above all of it, however, there exists a sort of intellectual skepticism about its permanent consequence. Outside the immediate relatives and friends directly affected by its daily efforts and antics, what possible difference can it make to the plethora of people in the world, or even the plethora of Invisibles in the skies, what specific things the ordinary individual does to compile the roster of his history, and even after such roster is compiled, what is there about it that should make the world bate its breath and remark on it in permanence? The desire to live and achieve and be notable is universal, but contrasted against it is the ironical perception that Nature itself is impersonal—or seems to be so—and the memory of even the most successful and famous persons lasts only a few generations or centuries at the most. Millions of people live and struggle and perish —only to be forgotten within two to five years after their funerals. It is the exceptional man or woman in any given community whose name is perpetuated a hundred years. The man or woman whose name is perpetuated a thousand years is a rarity. Can it be reasonably possible that the average man or woman is struggling and enduring through this Vale of Tears merely to get their names perpetuated a hundred or a thousand years? What a debatable compensation—especially when they consider they will not be on hand to enjoy such adulation. All of us know we don't do that. What then is the secret of the personal urge at work? Why does each of us subconsciously act as though he were the most important person in the universe—at least in his own esteem—and yet give way to periodic despair by conceding intellectually that he is of no more lasting importance in Nature than the aforesaid gnat in the sunset swarm that rises and falls on quiet air with its fellows?

It is something to look at, and not to treat lightly.

HE ANSWER to the paradox, when we begin to explore the eternal verities and the ageless wisdom opened to us when we are prepared to receive it, obviously lies in our mental limitations that are strictly of mortality. Look at it for a moment in this manner: Let's say a given rural community holds no more than five families. Each member of the family ensemble is known. There are, in totality, fifty-seven members of those family groups alive and related, and composing the life of the community as we recognize it. We have no difficulty recalling the five names Smith and Jones, and Brown, and Williams, and Neidiecomovitch. Five is a number our ordinary working minds can accommodate. Fifty-seven members to the Smith-Jones-Brown-Williams-Neidiecomovitch community are a little more difficult to remember. We know that each has sons and

daughters and aunts and uncles and cousins and nieces and nephews—and there is always the blonde Neidiecomovitch girl who forever hangs around the depot and flirts with the incoming Fuller brush-men. But we have difficulty recalling the faces and names of the individual members. We know that John Smith heads the Smith clan, and Bill Jones heads the Jones clan, and Bob Williams heads the Williams clan, and Jed Brown heads the Brown clan. We think the head of the Neidiecomovitch bunch is old Nicodemus, but we aren't positive; it may be his brother Sissocophagus. However, the five heads of the clans are individuals who at once stand out in mental pictures to us when their names are recalled. That, of course, is because we are operating our minds at five-man power. If we operated our minds at fifty-seven man-and-woman power, we would have just as clear pictures of the whole Smith-Jones-Brown-Williams-Neidiecomovitch community—but we don't. We say, therefore, that fifteen or twenty people tends to "confuse" us. We aren't deprecating the importance or individuality of the entire fifty-seven people in the said community; we are confessing we lack the mental perception to think of fifty-seven as we thought of the five who do the clan-heading.

Now multiply this situation by all the persons in a given metropolis, let's say New York. Manhattan is "big" because it holds one million times the Smith-Jones-Brown-Williams-Neidiecomovitch families of our rural community. Actually, however, New York is "big" because of the limitations of our minds to conceive them individually. The trouble isn't with New York that there are too many people running about and getting knocked down by traffic; the trouble lies in our mental restrictions, that keep us making the effort to think of six million persons with five-man and rural community recognitions ✠

Our mentalities aren't "developed" that facilely, and so we fuse all these six million Smith-Jones-Brown-Williams-Neidiecomovitch persons into a "mass population" and call it a "metropolitan area"—and we say immigration should be curtailed because so many people are piling in that the real estate can't accommodate them ✠

The ensemble is hopelessly beyond our limited conceiving, and generally speaking we don't like it. As a matter of fact, we suspect that with the numbers increasing, some of them may even be Bolsheviks, planning to overthrow the government. What we don't like actually, of course, is our own inability to individualize more than five persons at one time. We criticize and castigate ourselves in terms of the teeming millions that compose the American melting pot—that doesn't melt.
¶Now take that same exposition and apply it to the "billions" overrunning the earth, and we retire in hopeless and insufferable defeat. Nobody can possibly "keep track" of so many human entities, therefore we as can-

didate-receivers are lost in the shuffle—worse luck! Only we're not. We're no more lost in any shuffle than we would be lost standing in the center of Main Street —or what passes for Main Street—in Hillsboro and nodding to John Smith, Bill Jones, Jed Brown, or Nicodemus or Sissocophagus Neidiecomovitch. What we're lost in, in the case of Manhattan or the world population, is the amazing microcosm of our own one-cell minds. And that there might be, in the universe, wits big enough and powerful enough to stand in the middle of Broadway and recognize and nod to every last Smith and Jones and Brown and Williams and both the senior Neidiecomovitches who happen to pass either north or south, fills us with a sort of skeptical facetiousness. Because we couldn't do it, no one could do it, therefore we reason it couldn't be done. Because it couldn't be done, there is no one to do it. Therefore Nature is impersonal and life is a desert drear, without meaning or objective.
¶ What we tend to find out in the study of the Higher Wisdom is: that just as a hill-billy Smith mother who had given birth to twenty-two children, could recall the names and personalities of every last one without the slightest difficulty or possession of any "super-brains", so the Great Author of us all operates under no mortal limitation in respect to "remembering" us. And we know this privately in our hearts—or rather our emotions—even though we scoff at it when considered by our intellects. How do I know? I know it not only

by the "instinctive" feeling that I experience—and that you experience—that I am by no means lost in Cosmos any more than you are lost in Cosmos, but I find myself going back again and again to a communication that Mary and I recorded on the 11th day of December, 1928, when I asked the Great Teacher an all-important question, and got what was to me an all-important answer. "Master," I said, "what is the one greatest message that we can convey to the current human race as coming from You, the significance of your communications above all other significances, that we can make the cornerstone of all our preachments in this wisdom in the years that lie ahead?"

And the answer came back at once, so electric, so vital, and so different from what I had expected, that it is almost sacrilegious to revert to our old friend Subconscious Mind as possibly being its origin—

"THE FACT that every life, no matter how humble, no matter how tragic, no matter how broken or thwarted, has a meaning and an Inner Glory and is precious in My sight!"

Every life, mark you! Yours and mine and the President's and the local alderman's and the bum's who held you up for a dime last night to buy himself a cup of coffee, and the King of England's, and the Neidiecomovitch girl's who flirts with the salesmen at the depot in

Hillsboro, and the policeman's who gives you a ticket for driving sixty an hour through a thirty-mile zone. All their lives are of equal consequence in the estimate of the Great Avatar who is near us and about us here at the beginning of the Aquarian Month to awaken us to the real plan of salvation proceeding to fruition for every last mother's son and father's daughter of us. NONE ARE LEFT OUT. The Plan encompasses the complete totality of us. And when viewed in such light, we begin to understand why we sincerely and devotedly love the Elder Brother. He isn't choosing persons and preferring some personalities to other personalities. He isn't indicting some of us as saved and others of us as damned. The program afoot is bigger and vaster and more splendorful than that. Apparently He loves all of us, and is concerned with all of us, BECAUSE WE ARE POSSESSORS OF CONSCIOUS LIFE. That is the qualification by which we merit attention—not whether we were sired by the Astorbilts or were educated at Eton or had a rich uncle die and leave us ten million dollars, but whether we are suffering, struggling, learning mortal souls, going up the great escalator of life to the higher floors of radiant intelligence where our intellects expand to where we can grasp the six million Smiths, Joneses, Browns, Williams and Neidiecomovitches—or the two billion Smiths, Joneses, Browns, Williamses and Neidiecomovitches—as easily as we now stand in the center of Main Street, Hillsboro, and nod to the five heads of the clans who make up the local population en toto.

Already He possesses the expansion of intellect to know us and recognize us, whether we dwell in Hillsboro ourselves, or New York or Aberdeen or Odessa or Peking. Being the Universal Elder Brother to all of us, He knows us as He would know us if we were one of the Smith woman's twenty-two children, of which He was first-born. He has the intellect to do that. And when we retire in a sort of hopeless despair, and lament that we are of no particular consequence in the world because there are two billion other human beings overrunning the earthly stage amid which we are lost in the shuffle, all we are indicting truly is our own current intellectual limitation, our Brain Power so to speak, that at present can't recognize more than five faces distinctly in this Hillsboro of the world.

It is as simple as that.

IF ONE thing stands out to me in all this supernal teaching above every other thing, it is this single staggering fact: having had our psyches originally created—or brought into individual being—at the commencement of our cosmic existence, it is the Long Record of what we have done, are doing, and will do, with this unit of consciousness that is ourselves, that really decides our eternal cosmic worth—not the silly

business of whether we winked at Deacon Allen's wife in church last Sunday, or short-changed the Higgins woman on a pound of sugar two years ago Easter, or looked upon the wine when it was red and let it sting us like a serpent and bite us like an adder at Cousin Sally's wedding, when we got into a fight with the garage mechanic from Ebbensville and broke up the festivities by punching his eye.

Life is bigger than all this. The eternal program is finer and sweeter and vaster, and FAIRER to all of us who never have had a real chance anyhow to be the real people we have wished to be in our hearts.

This Christ whom we worship is not a petty god—and you notice I print it god and not God. He is the Example Character, sent or come to us to emulate, just to prove to us that He can be emulated. He rarely rebukes. What He does is Suggest. We can take fifty lifetimes, apparently, to consider or accept His suggestions, but we will do it in the end because we'll be left behind in the cosmic graduation if we don't.

This the thing is, that theology doesn't tell us.

Theology binds the prospect down hard and fast and inhumanly intolerant. It says, Believe on the Lord Jesus Christ and thou shalt be saved; refuse to believe on Him and thou shalt be damned.

The Elder Brother Himself, when we succeed in getting into conscious communication with Him, says nothing of the sort. He says, "I come unto the world to give it the example of My life. Follow in My footsteps and you know spiritual improvement and peace of mind. I don't save you from a wrathful God; I show you the pattern and give you the enlightenment whereby you save yourselves from a wrathful Self. There is no sentimentality in it. There is merely common sense in it. The moment you pattern your life on My life, you become illustrious and important and prosperous and beloved. It is My job in this mortal universe to exhibit to you the type of personality you should have acquired by the time you're ready to quit coming back to it and go on into more wonderful areas of Radiance that is the true Heaven."

But meantime He's concerned in all of us, and looks upon our worldly stations in life as a classroom for our particular and peculiar personalities where we're learning something special that we require to learn to render us in the ultimate more like Himself.

This, to my way of regarding it, is a religion that has heart and soul and divinity in it—a religion that is worth regarding with loving reverence. This eternal clubbing over the pate that humanity has suffered up the past two thousand years, to make it fit to enter Heaven, is medieval and vengeful, and belongs back in a day when the authorities sought to make people good by frying them at the stake.

No man was ever made good by compelling him to suffer torture! He may succumb to the dictates of the torturers, but he hates them with a venomous hatred in his heart.

T IS time to bring humanity an entirely remodeled concept of the Christian faith, and introduce this Man of Nazareth to the modern world as an Elder Brother—precisely what He calls Himself—who stands ready to help and encourage as a loving older brother would, and does, those of His family and relatives who need what He is able to supply them.

The big thing we've got to alter our concepts to grasp and assimilate is this—

WE ARE ALL CHRISTS IN SCHOOL!

What does it matter if certain classrooms are difficult to experience? The fact that they're difficult demonstrates that we are deficient in what they have to teach us, else they wouldn't be difficult.

The world has gone forward blindly, almost hopelessly, over the past twenty centuries, accepting such depictions of the Elder Brother as a Hebraic sail-maker named Paul thought fit to give it. Paul did a fairly good job, considering his times and limitations. But the world has progressed since Paul's day. We are coming out into the illuminations of a new celestial month, and the Elder Brother proceeds to shine forth to us as a wholly different personage than St. Paul bethought Him ⚜

We are subtracting nothing of the divinity and faith of the Christian religion, to bring to humanity the concept of the REAL Elder Brother as we in these modern times are electrically discovering Him. We are saying to these times: Forget your Hebraic ideas of vengeance in all this Deity business and try to grasp from His words and preachments the real Elder Brother as he is.
¶ If He has no evidences of vengeance in HIS makeup, why need we pay homage to any God of Vengeance whom He regards as Father? As a matter of fact, He tells us specifically that to think of the Personage whom He regards as Father as being vengeful, is to deal in blasphemy ☩
THE ANCIENT OF DAYS IN THE UNIVERSE IS AN AUGMENTED AND GLORIFIED CHRIST, A HUNDRED TIMES MORE UNDERSTANDING AND COMPASSIONATE THAN THE MAN OF NAZARETH EVER HOPED TO BE!
This is the "God" of popular tradition and superstition, and it now begins to be apparent that if we neglect to know Him as He is we are but inhibiting ourselves even worse than we are at present, when our one-cell intellects can't recognize more than five clan-heads in Main Street, Hillsboro.
This too is something to think about!

HEARD the supernal Sages of the past tell me there was no God but Spirit in the opening lectures of this clairaudient instruction, and yet I heard the Elder Brother refer constantly to the "Father", and I challenged the contradiction. If there were no "God" but Spirit, who or what, then, was the Being whom the Elder Brother contended He served as "son"?
¶ Thus on the 11th day of December, 1928, I had the ensuing paper dictated in the Transcendent Writing, which cleared the mystery for good—and I have been properly respectful ever since toward the wisdom of the sages, who committed no fault in using the nomenclature they did.
Personally, glancing back over twenty years of these supernal recordings, I know of no "message" in my books—and I have preserved every scrap of writing scrupulously—that surpasses in awe and majesty the communication I now intend to print in this volume, entitled "The Ancient of Days" . .
Let alone whether Sirius, or its gigantic planet, is the truthful Seat of the Godhead, from which man-spirits made some sort of migration back in Miocene times, this delineation of who and what the Ancient of Days is, does rationalize the Being whom men venerate as Jehovah. I give you the communication for what you consider it worth to your own evolving and developing intellect

Remember, we are all of us learning in a respectful spirit in these discourses, accepting only that which reconciles with our intellects and common sense. Knowing the need of all of us for clarification of these terms "God" and "Spirit" and "Father", the following was submitted for my consideration, and has filled my own soul with peace and understanding ever since the night that a visiting Great Soul bespoke it . .

THE REVELATION

The Ancient of Days

MY DEARLY BELOVED:

THERE are things to be known that have a bearing on your stay in flesh; I tell you of some of them. I come to you, teaching you, that ye may be wise.

Know that men have often said that I am Son of God, meaning a literal Father dwelling in a literal heaven, surrounded by His angels and judging men at the end of life according to their deeds. That, of course, is a sort of compromise between the truth and what they would believe of their own pictures in form, not knowing how to picture the abstract. But this is important—

¶There are those amongst us, in flesh and out of it, who have seen what no man hath seen. They have penetrated to vast distances spiritually and perceived there sights and sounds beyond earthly comprehension. They have returned to earth to tell of those experiences, to relate what happened to them of their mental senses. They have pictured to those below them on the earth-plane a series of dramas, apparently occurring within their inspection in the times of their visitations. These have taken form and become apparent to earthly brains as the expressions of common theology.

Now I tell you the truth about these things, that ye may

be wise above your generation and leaders of your groups. Repeat it unto them circumspectly for verily it transcendeth their knowledge of the present.

There is no Father, as hath been told you, excepting that out of the Infinite cometh Reason by a process that hath in it creation as ye know it. This Reason is the Voice of Creation, telling men born and unborn of vast mysteries ⚜

These mysteries, My beloved, are choice of selection. By that I mean, they encompass circumstances that cannot be interpreted excepting as mankind compare them with the knowledge which he hath in his own experience ⚜

But this Voice of Reason is more than argument. It hath in it potencies which take form in Thought . .

I SPEAK unto you with wisdom when I say that all of us are Thoughts manifesting in so-called Matter, which itself is thought—not a projection of the intellect but a conceiving of things as they might be, wherefore they are.

By this I mean, Thought is of eternity before Matter, being all that there is the Cosmos.

The Cosmos in turn is Thought. I tell you it began to manifest in Matter trillions of millennia ago in earthly time for a purpose. It was impossible to conceive, even emotionally, without form of some kind to give Thought character and measurement.

When I tell you that the Earth Plane, and mortal life, is but a type of Thought-measurement, I explain life closer to truth than in any other way or by any other measurement

Life is the projection of Thought, indeed, but it is Thought projecting in terms of quantities for measurement of itself as valuation of its own attributes.

By this I mean that life hath in it the essence of Thought whilst at the same time it IS Thought: this I perceive ye do know.

When I speak of the Father, therefore, I speak verily of one who ruleth the Host of All Thought Streams: a spirit so aged that no man knoweth Its identity or antiquity

This Spirit, in power, is beyond even My conceiving, even as I was temporarily beyond your conceiving whilst in mortal flesh.

This Spirit existeth and endureth, older I say than any known to the Host of those of whom I have knowledge. He is not God as men conceive God. Nevertheless, He is so wise in His conceiving that His power transcendeth that of any spirit projected onto any plane of which we have wisdom.

WHEN I say that I am Son of God and refer to the Father, invariably I refer to this Spirit—because with Him I am in touch and know no greater beyond Him

I TELL YOU, BELOVED, I BELIEVE OTHERS TO BE BEYOND HIM, but of them I have no knowledge and probably never will have knowledge, THEY EVER RECEDING AS WE APPROACH THEM.

When I say unto you, therefore, that the Father existeth, and yet I say there is no God but Thought, I do not speak a paradox nor fabricate in either case.

We have spirits here with us on This Side so powerful of knowledge, concept, and constructive emotionalism, that they do transcend even Myself who am given Earth as My temporary ruling-place. These Spirits are known to Me intimately, and to you when you are out of flesh.

¶This happeneth, however, . . these Infinite Spirits, for I call them such, greater in power than any known to mortal ken, have control of the universe as men know it. They are omnipotent and omnipresent in the world and in the universe, ruling it by Thought Projection and enabling it to function.

I have come among men for this purpose time and time again, not to manifest omnipotence, for omnipotence is ever relative and even the Ruler of the Host hath it not, strictly speaking, but I have come among men to teach them something higher than that which they perceive in this travail that is of earth.

I have shown them the Way, the Truth, and the Light —particularly the Light.

I have come as instructor, not as ruler, although by My instruction do I rule. I have come into flesh times beyond count, manifesting unto men that which they may attain even in blinded and handicapped concepts of the present 🞽

Now we come to this situation—

Man hath said there is no God, and of truth this is so, for God in truth is Thought Incarnate. But in their saying they have meant this: There is no ruler to Whom we are accountable. But in such concept, I tell you they have erred.

Truly there are twenty million rulers to whom they are accountable, for each species and kind hath its rulers to whom they are accountable, whether on plane of earth or planets off in decimal Space.

DO YOU accept, and make a cornerstone of your thinking, that humankind as ye know it is not the only manifestation of mortality that existeth. Planets beyond your ken have their species and races and cohorts and potentates, dwelling in all sorts and conditions of livinghood and making practice of their talents according to their development of intellect. Verily animals are some of these, though far, far down upon the scale of intelligence, so far down that whole groups are required to express one psyche.

What I would tell you tonight is this—

There is One God in respect to the concernment that there is a ruler of the planetary systems. This Ruler,

I say, is an old, old spirit, older than any of which we have knowledge.

His comings and goings are marked by vast cataclysms, so that stars perish and reassemble in His presence. Verily is He incarnate in the universe as ye do know the universe of sight and sound. Yet doth He dwell in presence on a far, far planet, greater in extent than your minds can encompass.

I go unto Him for instruction at intervals—a Living Entity who hath so great a power that for Him to speak is for creation to consummate. But Gods hath He in turn beyond Him, of similar structure, vastness, and incomprehensibility, for the universe hath no end in majesty ☼

We must conceive these things to get our errand clear to us. Mayhap the day arriveth when we too shall be so great that world systems are born at our pronouncing, but that altereth not the fact that there dwelleth in Infinity a Creature and a Creation of such vastness of concept that He knoweth the comings and goings of planets as doves in a cage that is hung in a window.

Mark this well, My beloved: He hath knowledge of all of you even as I have knowledge of all of you. He saith to Me nightly: What of Thy fellowship with those who do dwell with Thee upon the planet Earth, and the concepts thereof in Thought? Have those who do compose it kept faith with Thee? Do they please Thee? Great shall be their reward in knowledge if they do perform at Thy desire and in fulfillment of Thine instruction.

I say unto Him: Verily, Father, is it so. Report I progress day unto day. Night unto night seeth the action advanced whereby the Man Spirits cleave unto My principles, and advance in their knowledge of values of spirit ✠

MAKE NO mock of this, My beloved. A Spirit watcheth over Me even as I watch over My friends and compatriots in the work of raising mankind to knowledge—that he proceedeth upward, millennia by millennia ✠

Now mark this well: When cometh the time that we have completed our labors and man hath no longer need of this planet, this thing transpireth—

THE WORLD, I TELL YOU, DISTINTEGRATETH IN THOUGHT!

That is to say, out of the mouth of the Father cometh thunderings, declaring a new and more perfect location for humankind—a better prepared planet where men do dwell in a sort of fleshly concept that is higher toward perfection than that which now prevaileth, that they may learn other lessons not addicted to the pleasure-pain experience.

I tell you of this in another lesson, but this is acutely desirable for you to know:

The time cometh when men shall say, "There is no God

as we have known Him, not even celestial ruler of our group; we have no use for rulership for verily we rule ourselves; hoaxed have we been by priests and clergymen; all, all is theological vanity and humor wrongly placed in our concept. We have knowledge only of essences. These we rely on. Teach us not blasphemies, we implore you, of ourselves."

Say unto them, beloved: "Lo, it is not so! Verily we do have two rulers, He who was Jesus of Nazareth ruling you immediately and He who ruleth over the Order of which Jesus of Nazareth is member, in whose household He standeth well."

Transcribe this, My beloved, in pictures of gold within frames of silver. Tell it with diamonds as your pigments —for so important is it that men should know this that it transcendeth every debacle of reasoning wherein man is convicted.

WE HAVE known of old of this Ancient Ruling Spirit, but men have conceived of Him wrongly, calling Him God of wrath and torture, of unpleasant utterance and divine malediction. Verily, verily, there is falsehood in that.

Greater is He in beauty than ever I have shown Myself unto man, greater in understanding, greater in toleration, greater in infinite compassion, for verily hath He not encompassed the world in His bosom, and doth He not encompass it as these hours fly swiftly?

I would say unto you, beloved, we have an immediate Father so intimate that to think of Him is to know Him, and to live in flesh is to be part of His substance. Verily His incarnation is in the universe itself as ye do perceive it. That is His body and His flesh, though He dwell in addressable spirit a trillion miles afar. I would have you take this literally, no lesson being greater which I have taught you.

ALL UP and down men's ages have come those saying: We see not this God, this ancient ruler, this omnipresent One. In that we cannot point Him out, we proceed to deny Him. Verily, my beloved, they speak as children who have not received wisdom from logic and experience. And yet I tell you more—
When cometh the Host unto you, who are they, and whence come they? This I reveal to you likewise, knowing that merit of understanding is in it . .
Lo, there are millions unto trillions of essences in existence who have passed beyond all sense-planes as ye do understand them, but have not yet attained to incarnations in universes.
THEY ARE THE HOST . .
They are not as ye are, exactly. Verily are they great in concept of knowledge, and application of wisdom gained through experiencings. But I say this thing happeneth—
THEY HAVE FAILED TO PERFORM THAT

WHICH WOULD ENTITLE THEM TO CREATE FOR THEMSELVES THAT WHICH THEY WOULD INHABIT!

Lo, they too learn lessons, yet greater are their attainments than any in mortal concept. They do go to and fro, behested by this Ancient of Days, whom ye term the Father.

I teach you no mystery.

The Host hath performed, and doth perform, yet performeth it not adequately. Thus are those of it caught upon the horns of a dilemma. They do perceive their own inadequacies of attainment and yet are powerless to attain until they have come to that state wherein they perceive that they are the thing they should be. When that is attained, they go forward in concept, compiling worlds and dwelling within them.

WHENCE came the Father, you ask? I tell you that no man and no spirit knoweth excepting those who may be older than He in point of understanding.

So goeth it.

We are creatures of gradations in eternal time—and now do we come to the heart of our discourse.

Man hath a mission unto the Father, the true god of his species by point of seniority. The Father would have this performed. Even as an earthly father desireth that his sons be like him in attainments so doth he make them attentive to him, that he may give them wisdom. So would the Father desire that man-spirits should be like him in attainments of the mind and heart.

Consider this well, My beloved.

It hath been said of old: the fear of the Lord is the beginning of wisdom. I say unto you that loving the Father and being loved by Him is the commencement of eternal knowledge. What hath the phrase meant, the fear of the Lord is the beginning of wisdom? Not terror of Him, for that is blasphemous. Fear meaneth worry that whatever is perceived is not that which is conceived—understand ye this?

The fear of the Lord, therefore, or the Ancient of Days, is this: Worry deservedly that man's understanding faileth to encompass him, to man's detriment in wisdom.
¶ Mark this well: Men have knowledge of their creator in the days of their youth, for verily they remember those truths which they have lately brought over with them from the Thought Planes above the physical.

Men have no knowledge therefore of those principles of Creation that have wrought Thought itself into measurements of action, and never will they have it, even as I have it not, for verily, My beloved, it cannot exist.

Ye are creatures of temperament, therefore are ye human. But temperament transcendeth mortal coil and becometh divine reflection. When thus it cometh, it is the beginning of the end, for remember, this, the end, is the beginning and the beginning is the end, and therefore is there neither excepting in function. Would that

I could make you to see this as I see it, but dwelling in a world of Cause and Effect it is well-nigh impossible to reach the stage or plane where cause mergeth into effect and both are the same, revealing the solution of that which is at present a riddle.

Can I make this plain to you? Verily My heart beateth for you that ye have not the knowledge understandably. Presently ye do have it when your span of days be ended, though ye go into flesh again and again, each time forgetting it purposely.

Now I speak with authority when I say, tell not My people riddles. Make all plain to them which they will accept, with or without circumstances for validation. Teach those who would be taught. Instruct those who ask of you. Turn none away who come saying: Masters of the Wisdom ye do claim that ye be, tell us therefore the Why of this or that. Verily, beloved, tell them a thousand times till their ears do tire from hearing—for that is your mission, undertaken by each of you who love Me and would aid in My coming . .

THE SECOND COMING

THE SECOND COMING

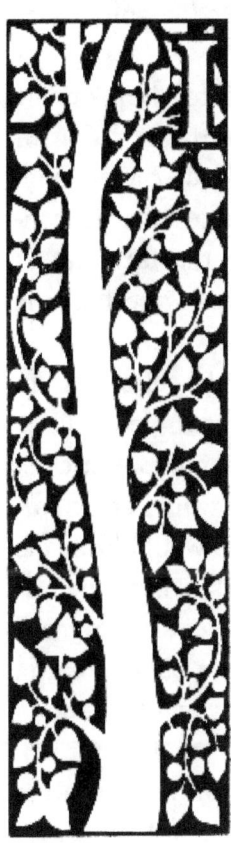

IT HAS ever been a watchword among Christian converts to await the Second Coming of Christ. The idea seems to have been from the first that some fine day, down here in modern times, a vast thunderstorm and earthquake would suddenly break on humanity, the heavens would be "rolled back as a scroll," and they should behold a resurrected Man of Nazareth descending down a splendorful stairway, to begin giving orders right and left for the regenerated of a world in which He reigns in dictatorial might for a thousand years, "putting all enemies under His feet." Well, while we're upon these sacred subjects and considering them intimately, supposing we look at this Second Coming as a literal event and see what it proposes.

A literal event engages all the powers of earth and air and materials and physical phenonena. So again we have the right to inquire into the tangible properties of such an occurrence and see to what extent the sacred writers have borrowed more from imagination and wishful thinking than from their reason and cognitions of the material means involved . .

St. John was supposed to have gone to sleep on the island of Patmos and received a clairvoyant vision of exactly what was to transpire when Jesus came again. But one of the first things we must take note of, considering St. John's clairvoyance, was the fact that in St. John's day, men weren't generally aware that the world was round.

If Jesus came back to earth, to take up the celestial scepter and reign over His kingdom—granted He could be intrigued into such a childish piece of pomp and ceremony—the place where He descended would be of paramount importance. Furthermore, we would have the reasonable and respectful right to ask where He expected to descend FROM, and what materials composed the stairway structure that lowered Him back to earth. Certainly it would be a fine thing to have all the motion picture and television cameras on the spot and catch this apex spectacle of the ages on film for the edification of future generations. But in the whole of it, we ought not to overlook the fact that if Jesus were to return to earth as St. John implies, then one-half to three-quarters of mankind are due to be denied a look at the exhibition.

¶ Remember, if this is a literal event that is due to come there are certain physical properties and behaviors of the earth as a planet that are going to raise considerable mischief with St. John's predicted ideas of it.

St. John, I repeat, didn't know that the earth was round; he didn't know, furthermore, that it turns from west to east at the rate of about one thousand miles per hour. Even if the returning Christ—and I speak with every respect—were to descend the divine stairway in fifteen minutes of footwork to get down, the terra firma under the bottom of the ladder—or stairway or escalator—would be two hundred and fifty miles removed from the spot where it was when the phenomenon started to happen. This motion of the earth as a planet is not only going to deny millions of people a view of the spectacle—it is bound to make havoc of the celestial descent as a literal structure. If the Second Coming were to begin in St. Louis, the earth would be turning away from it so fast that if it occupied fifteen minutes, the people of Kansas City would be the favored ones who came "in" for the finish. Meantime, all the good Christians in London, Paris, and cities overseas would be especially peeved against America for being favored with the spectacle, while they only heard about it by radio or cable.

It is a bad business to write a book—even a Book of Revelation—as being the last word in celestial occurrences, and not be an accomplished physicist in the action of natural processes.

 KNOW that in my own youth, I heard the story of the Second Coming as St. John describes it, and underwent no little intellectual distress as to how the thing could happen—a literal Christ returning to take up the scepter to rule a literal world by coming down a literal stairway from "heaven"—without considerable instability of the supporting materials, and a grievous shortsuiting of millions of good people in one hemisphere or the other who would want a look-see at the pageant and be disappointed by reason of the earth's rotundity. If the Second Coming happened in or around Jerusalem of the present, more than three-fourths of the earth's population would obtain no view of it— and why should they be thus penalized?

As a matter of fact, St. John's wish-fulfillment-dream seems to have been all that the reverend gentleman could call up at the moment, introducing the Prince of Peace to a future world that undoubtedly would welcome Him, without overexerting himself—St. John's overexerting himself—to check up much on the mechanical properties involved.

Not till I got deeply into this clairaudient instruction

did I have the matter straightened out to my satisfaction. And I don't mean the super-duper Stairway by which the Prince of Peace MIGHT return to this earth for a space to give authenticity to the whole Christian program ⚊

It involves, of course, going back to ordinary kitchen-garden fundamentals of psychics.

In the first place, we are required to ask ourselves in all sincerity whether the Man of Galilee ever went away from this planet, at His alleged ascension, and if so, WHERE? ⚊

We know from our researches into psychical phenomena, that the average human soul on quitting the body merely graduates into a fourth-dimensional area that is part of the three-dimensional area in which our material bodies operate. It it "right here with us" to all respects and purposes, but in a "Light Body" aspect that holds the mental faculties and not much else. Why then should we not expect the same to have been the Next-World condition of the Master Teacher? Why should He have mounted to any heavenly height to spend the forthcoming twenty centuries since His demise in Jerusalem? If this is His world, and He has had any sustaining interest in it, would He not have continued His spiritual sojourning in it?

This being reasonable, in the event that He decided to reenter it physically, would He not duplicate a performance we can see demonstrated in any psychical clinic in the nation any night when a good teleplasmic medium is available—to wit, gather materialistic atoms around his own supernal Light Body and thus become, to all intents and purposes, tangible and "real" to the faithful followers most desirous of having Him present on earth in the "flesh"?

Would that not be a literal Second Coming insofar as projecting Him into earthly conditions were concerned?
¶ Too bad, of course, that the Cecil B. DeMille super-duper spectacle is denied us, but what actual difference does it make if we have Him back here with us, known for whom He is? The vital business interesting us is, what does He propose to do when He gets here, and is this "take His scepter and reign for a thousand years" another literal circumstance in earthly affairs or merely a symbolic word-picture of the Christ-Spirit arriving among men in such form that It alters the aspects of their secular institutions and puts authenticity into the whole prognostication of divine intervention in mundane affairs?

ARLY in all this clairaudient instruction, I began to have inklings recorded of a "miracle" that was ultimately to take place in human society, speaking figuratively, when the millions of the world's population were to have demonstrated that the Prince of Peace was by no manner of means a mere allegorical figure but a very real Personality. What was the nature of this Miracle? I slowly discerned that it had something to do with the return of the Man Christ into physical form and His taking of His offices as secular ruler of the universe and arbiter of international institutions. But mark this well—

He by no means seemed to propose assuming this authority with the mortal arrogance of any celestial Hitler or Roosevelt. Nor did I gather that He was to become President of any United Nations, speak over the radio, toss out baseballs at World Series sporting events, or commandeer trains at the taxpayer's expense and tour the forty-eight American States making asinine speeches from rear platforms.

What I did seem to gather from the intelligence conveyed to me was, that a time was in prospect when the nations of the earth would come up to the threshold of a third World War, hemisphere pitted against hemisphere, and the "abomination of desolation"—evidently the devastation resulting from a contest of atom and hydrogen bombs—readied to break on mankind. Hundreds of statesmen would be assembled in an international conference to decide on, or reject, this catastrophe —here or in Europe would be immaterial. In such a fraught stage in the world's affairs, the assembled statesmen would suddenly behold a blinding vision of supernal radiance and the Man of Galilee would show Himself for What and Who He was . . in a stupendous display of Light Vibrations that should give them the jitters for a year and a day. In other words, He would do what any ordinary human person might do, if he had the teleplasm available, materialize before men with an exhibit of what He was in materialized and glorified form, and convince them by such a visual exhibit that Christianity is no intellectual or sentimental byplay. The Man of Galilee is REAL and the designation of Himself as "ruler" of the nations is no dogmatic fol-de-rol ☙

That would be a Second Coming that would combat no laws of mundane physics and call for no explanations of celestial "stairways" whose bases were planted on a moving planetary surface hurling eastward at a thousand miles an hour.

Again the delineations made the soundest part of sense.
¶ I had had a sincere and devout Episcopalian clergyman, a chaplain in World War I, assure me in all sober conviction that he had often seen the Man of Nazareth moving among the wounded and easing the agonies of the dying, in a subdued radiance of person that could

not be mistaken. I had had dozens of attestments from no less sincere people, that they had witnessed aspects of the Christ Personality in sick rooms and about deathbeds—and here was I, obtaining clairaudient messages from some Stupendous Personality who was assuring me of my own part in a phase of social instruction that I could by no means repudiate. If all these things had a basis in truth, and the Teacher of Nazareth were already upon this earth-plane, what sort of Cecil B. DeMille mumbo-jumbo had St. John described, that the Teacher of Nazareth was coming down some glorified staircase at some vague future time, to "take His scepter"? I began to give serious attention to this "Miracle" that was implied in my own clairaudient instruction, and to learn all about it that was offered.

The general gist of the intelligence seemed to be: that there were incarnate in life some 144,000 of the very elect of the Avatar's aides, who went from life to life and from body to body, seeking ways and means in every generation of advancing His work and principles among men. They were the ones who counseled and instructed and helped and interpreted the more abstruse aspects of Christian doctrine—though in many lives they had been martyred for their efforts.

They were fairly well all incarnated in this present state of the world's affairs, and were generally waiting for Him to reach the moment when He would come voluntarily into "the grinding and groaning of atoms" for this

supernal display of avatar personality. But it would be upon them that the advancement of Christian doctrine —the true Christian doctrine—rested when He had displayed Himself as being a literal personage with a literal mission to execute.
And how would He execute it?
He would execute it through the aides and servants who were already incarnate in mortal life, apprising THEM of what had to be done, and how they should do it, to achieve the maximum of social regeneration in the thousand years that were being ushered in by this supernal display on His part . .

 HAVE learned nothing in all of this sacred clairvoyant instruction that indicates that this Master Teacher and Exemplar is due to turn dictator, use miraculous means for getting His dictates honored, and crack anyone over the pate with a celestially stuffed club if he fails to perform as the Great Avatar directs. That is not His mission, and He would be the first to repudiate the use of Force to make men "good" in the light of all the preachments He has given us to date, that it is Experience and naught else that truly makes men good to remain good . . the recognition that only as we do unto others as we would be done by, do we get payments which we desire to our spirits, in kind ⚘
The Great Teacher of Galilee does not seem to be the

sort of Dictator who requires a regiment of Storm Troopers to effect His commands—He gives attestment of His continuing Personality to those who voluntarily do His work among men, and demonstrates that Christianity is not a Voltarian myth; it is a vital and constructive force by which men escape all the toils and troubles to which they are heirs in earthly life.

Even after His Second Coming, He will undoubtedly depend upon earnest disciples to get the work done—or accomplished—for which He came to this earth planet untold aeons in the past.

He would only cheapen Himself by setting Himself up as a political potentate and laying down orders for the conduct of society which men were by no means ready to obey without force to compel them.

The Great Teacher, I perceive, deludes neither Himself nor His disciples, by the threaten use of Force.

You are good because you want to be good—because it profits you most to be good—not because someone who had gloriously materialized in a light body waves fiery torches about your head and pronounces that you must be good or you get grievously burned by the flames they exude.

It is well to bear the physical possibilities of the Second Coming in mind, when considering not only this stupendous religious event but the character of the Teacher Himself who comes. There are veiled alludings in one communication after another that I received as early as twenty years ago, to the symbolism: "Thirteen is the number; seven times seven is the number of days." That puzzled me so much that I sought clarification whenever opportunity offered. Finally I decided that the mystical Appearance was to take place thirteen times over a period of forty-nine literal days, and probably in thirteen different countries or capitals of the earth, so that all men might be aware of what was occurring. Mind you, I am publishing this suggestion only as an assumption. I do not KNOW and I do not claim that I know. I am merely drawing logical conclusions from such text as has been given me.

A Second Coming occurring after this pattern would solve the quandary of the earth's rotundity and rotation, and have the effect of complying with natural law. It would likewise comply with certain teleplasmic facts we feel we have determined by clinics in the great modern psychical societies.

That the Great Avatar, I say, would descend to the status of an earthly potentate or political executive, giving audiences to statesmen, keeping executive hours, making trips and speeches attendant on his political function, signing decrees, becoming in essence a mortal official burdened or harassed with the petty details of his position, is both degrading and absurd to contemplate. Neither do I hold with many good religionists that He would confine Himself to endless consultations with the heads of various church organizations throughout the world, and remain content with working through them to bring in the celebrated "reign of righteousness". At once vast bureaucratic jealousies between creed and creed, between Catholicism and Protestantism, between Christian and "heathen" would ensue. He might be accused of a partisan favoritism. All would be turmoil and controversy and rancor and antagonism, defeating the ends He was seeking to establish.

We have to apply ourselves to the communications that constitute the splendorful and informative background of this Enlightenment, and draw our own conclusions as to their significance, before we can say anything about this Event of the Ages with assurance. However, I mention it here in that it does seem to tie into this cosmic proposition of reclaiming the sons of earth from what we can describe as their ancient sodomic heritage. Confirmation that the Great Avatar is here amongst them, that He had been seen of eye and heard of ear, should introduce an universal interest in His resumed ministry on earth and an earnest exploration into its awesome premise that altered the thinking of the whole world upon subjects generally regarded as religious. The Reign of Righteousness should result, not from fiats uttered or enforced against evil doers, but from altered concepts of morality and ethics gained by the average man in the street when he has it brought home to him that the Christ who underwent crucifixion nineteen hundred and twenty years bygone is a

Very Real Personage in the current age and day and by no means the mythical or allegorical character that too many sects depict Him.

Apropos of this Phenomenal Return, I append hereunto a paper received upon the 7th of March, 1929, which you can read as I transcribed it and draw such conclusions as you please. I am pledging nothing in all this, I am offering nothing but a sharing with you of that which was projected into my own thinking for spiritual consideration. You are at liberty to read into it—or out of it—what you please. In my book of early scripts I find this particular revelation titled "Once Long Ago Did We Talk Thus in a Garden".

Will you get out of it what I got out of it?

THE REVELATION

A Talk in a Garden

MY DEAR ONES:

PEACE be unto you this night as we commune again.

I am desirous of instructing you in more mysteries, yet cometh a time when ye shall know them by your sense. Tonight I tell you regarding the future, and the details of the Miracle . .

Know that men do conspire together to slay My Goodly Company. They do connive to make wars and tumults among peoples that they may take profit of purse. They are an abomination to the Host of Higher Ones who ever seek man's good if he will have it. Know that I come to thwart them and confound them in the sight of posterity. Know that they shall face Me and My servants and be of chagrin and dismay, saying, We did not know, Master, when they did know well. I come to make mock of their activities and assume My pledged place as Counsellor to the nations.

Behold, My beloved, I shall have My vice-regents in that day and men shall follow them as now they profess to follow Me in words. Verily they shall say amongst themselves: These are the true rulers of the Church of God ☨

Know that these vice-regents, now mortal men of earth, heavenly in spirit, have been led through many vicissitudes for such leadership. Know that these have been the true cornerstones of My Church indeed, and those who so profess of present time shall be stricken into silence.

Now, My beloved, I would have speech with you in connection with this Miracle . .

MY SERVANTS, I say, have ever been sorely tried, as I too have known trial. They have clung to their ideals of Me though great forces waged unhallowed war against them. Yet have they seen the future from trend of event. Know that I have heard the cries of My servants' hearts upon a thousand nights and stood without their doors of spirit, awaiting the word of admittance. Know that I have seen their blunders of childhood with a smile. Know that I have witnessed their errors of young manhood and womanhood with a sigh. Know that I have seen them defenseless early, and thrown about and around them the blanket of My protection. But I have beheld their goodly works from day to day and knew them as My beloved of old, struggling through mists to reach My side. Know that even today they are so struggling, but the mists are now but webs of gossamer that shall presently be burned before the sun of righteousness.

Know that I have kept my pact. Know that I have told

My Father that we are ready for the Mission presently when we are come into full knowledge and cognizance, each of the other. From many lands and climes I call those who are mine. We do journey into sunrise with all souls of goodly works.

Know that I have drawn strength from My Father which I send unto My vice-regents, that their awakening may progress and be presently complete.

Now, My beloved, see ye not that we must ever be of single mind and purpose? The time telleth, the time witnesseth, the time maketh proof that My love is omnipotent ⚜

Ye have been honest in wanting the Veil rent asunder, but there have been reasons for it to hang between us for yet a little while. Knowledge cometh swiftly, wisdom groweth hourly, men are not made to see the Light too quickly lest damage result to that which they call their vision.

Ye, My servants, wherever My words find you, have been coming from the darkness of many earthly sojourns. Ye are blinded by the Light. It is the blinding from such light that amazeth you, not the fact that Light blazeth.

We are approaching an era of brilliance when the world shall shine with the Father's glory and mankind be ennobled; we are coming to eternal magnificence, I tell you, manifest in physical triumph over Darkness of Spirit ⚜

Accustom your eyes to the Light, My beloved. I am Its matter and Its core.

Now I speak of the instrumentalities we employ to wing ourselves to such realization of earthly divinities ☥ Harken while I make these clear to you—

MEN there are who would follow Me if they had but a sign that I was literal of person; they are lost sheep whom I pity and suffer with. Men there are who would follow Me if they could but worship Mammon without great inconvenience; they are goats of a sort who do not know that they have naught in common with My sheep excepting the forms thereof—they know not the true spiritualities that make creatures of Darkness divine.

Men there are who would have Me only at the price of earthly aggrandizement; they would follow where I lead if it but be to their renown; they are too silly to merit our speech. Men there are who will have none of Me unless I compensate them with reward; these men I scorn.

Men there are who will have none of Me until I show Myself more powerful than any earthly potentate and overthrow all governments built upon guile; they are rulers in a house of turmoil who seek order from disorder but know not where to turn for counsel; these I scorn not, but truly they must learn to live by their humbleness ☥

Lastly, men there are who shun Me and avoid Me, saying: Even with proof we believe on Him not. These go their way to the Pit of Forgetfulness, I tell you, there to dwell throughout eternity, the Everlasting Nameless. Be advised, the world hath need of all, beloved, but the last. We are come unto all men but the last. We are making the offering of ourselves to all but those who spit upon us when we would help and save them.

Know that we would love them but they want not our love. I repeat, we would save them but of their wills they choose the Pit. Verily we would hold out Hope to them, but Hope they spurn brutishly.

Beloved, be warned: The world doth not yet know Me and My household as presently it shall. It will not at first believe that we are returned unto it in flesh. Of you it will say, Were these not humble fishermen in the seas of great humanity? Of Me it will say, Was not this a mere spinner of tapestries showing hope rising unto hope, yet having no substance? Of both of us it will say: Were these not blasphemers who stood before multitudes and bragged of their sanctities?

In the Day of the Miracle, I tell you, men will gather together to ask of those who call themselves religious leaders: What meaneth it?

Some will say: Here are prophets who do magic. Some will say: Here are magicians who do prophesy. Some will ask: Were these not fishermen and painters of divine tapestries for notorieties? Whence cometh such power excepting from the Lord of Darkness? Some will cry: Let us stone them! Some will whisper: Let us imprison them lest they inflame the ignorant to seditions. Some will say: Let us be of smiling countenance until we learn the mystery, then do we make similar mysteries ourselves.

But some will say: These are Sons of God indeed; let us bow down and worship them lest destruction erase us. Think of these many times in future, Beloved, before the Miracle happeneth. Be of worthy meditation on them that ye may be aware of all types and classes. Now I tell you how to treat of them—

THOSE who love us, we protect; we show them the Light, we give them the Sign, we open the doors of their hearts and pass within, and dwell with them, and they with us. Truly we shall know them. Truly are they of the Goodly Company who but ask us for candles to light them to eternity. Even now, I say unto you, we embrace them from afar. What then shall be our joy when we gather in the midst of them?

Those who do make pretense of loving us until they inherit the secrets of our strength, we endure. Mayhap cometh to them some inkling of the truth that telleth them they are of the Company although they know it not. Mayhap they see in us relationships. Lo, seeking us falsely, they find us in truth.

Those who say: These are prophets but not of God,

let us even so tolerate. They too acquire learning when opportunity openeth and showeth them their blindness.
¶ Those who say, Were these not formerly fishers in small waters, humble women and men going about their errands and speaking of great matters as by a whimsy? truly shall they be converted who ask it when they see our divinity arising above all earthly handicap and manifesting gloriously on high planes of Spirit. Know that they shall be converted by the thought that even the Lord's anointed have come up through flesh, precisely like themselves. Know that we shall embrace them and love them and help them for their incredulity for were we not incredulous once ourselves, and perplexed as they are perplexed?

They who would destroy us as being of Lucifer shall not be tolerated, I tell you. The Host will convince them of their error or allow them to plunge to Long Death in forgetfulness.

Make no mistake, we are but working within the vineyard of the Father, gathering His fruits. Let no makers of abominations, spiritual, mental, or physical, attempt to thwart the workers in that vineyard.

And woe unto those who do use force against us! Tongues as of fire shall wither them, I tell you. Of those who would have no part of us, our speech passeth by ☙

Ever in men's hearts, I tell you, is hunger after solutions of that which men call mysteries. We are come to

show them the greatest in life: Who are we? Whence came we? Whither go we? Verily princes would give thrones to have such quandaries answered.
Know that we are come to forever tell mankind that the Cycle of Life closeth upon this planet, that it endureth here not forever, that the Father receiveth them after Time that hath an ending, that they must cease their displeasing conduct and enter His portals with obedience and respect, or forever afterward He knoweth them not.

BE YE advised: We are teachers and instructors of humanity. We do light the way for journeys into more and more resplendent heights, and our lamps go not out. Mankind hath the privilege of knowing for the final time that the Father receiveth him unto His bosom. Mankind hath the chance to restore himself back into those star worlds from which he wandered, and resume the lost splendor of ages in the past. This cometh not in a twinkling, beloved, yet nonetheless it cometh ✥
Men have the opportunity to acknowledge us as master and disciples of many numbers, doing good among them for their redemption. Woe unto the world if it receiveth us not a second time! Woe unto those whom we know in advance will spurn us! Waste not your compassion upon them, I tell you, for behold they are not worthy to receive it. We are here among men, sent

unto them to show that flesh is divine when inhabited by divinity and that divinity may subscribe to flesh, even flesh of mortal human.

We are come to show humankind that the life which inhabiteth flesh is the Godhead when ennobled above beasthood. We are come to make men realize that life is more than meat and drink and making merry; verily it is more than work and trade and taking usury.

Life, I tell you, is spiritual!

Life is nobility of character made manifest in act and award of merit. Life is the Godhead come to the planet Earth in individual particles called Souls who do good and orderly acts to externalize their heritage.

Be advised, My beloved: Once, long ago, we did talk thus in a Garden! Once did we speak of such mysteries when those who spoke them knew not they would one day find them in the lips of a hundred million worshipers ☙

Once did we come to a spring of cooling water and pause there drinking, and remarking on the thirst of humankind. Once did we see the multitude hungry and fed them, and gathered the fragments, and when the feast was done we did discuss these matters. Think ye we shall not go back again in memory down future ages and recall our present contacts and beseechments?

¶ O My Beloved, have endurance! We are writers of tales and sawyers of timbers. Verily we shall write epistles unto the Father and raise dwellings of marble as homes for His people! Know that the Goodly Company gathereth, that My spirit hovereth anew above its earthly heads. Know that I go to keep communion with them, and a covenant with them, and that presently all shall know one another for the brethren whom they are . . Now I tell you of the Miracle—

THE WORLD knoweth not My true servants' identities. It considereth them men and women who have brains of promise and fertility. But My servants know they are more than men and women. They are divine of essence, making missions to earth for the Father and Myself. This is their shibboleth: that the Father holdeth them to an accounting for their responsibilities in this progressing world!
I have redeemed it from annihilation. They are to take it a long step further in that Progress toward Perfection. Know then and be advised: When the time draweth nigh for the Miracle to happen, great will be the confusion amongst the nations. People shall be hostile; they shall make mock treaties of peace, having war in their hearts. They shall commit violations of pledged word and great trespass of territories.
In the days ahead shall come great disturbances of Nature; great cataclysms shall fill men's hearts with alarm; great international rumblings shall be felt; science shall run riot; nation and nation shall suffer in common from burnings and floods and famines and exhaustions.

There shall be minor wars. The sons of men shall cry Peace! yet behold no peace cometh.

These are signs and omens.

I say unto you that men now await the voice of one whom they know not, excepting he be of Me. Men are asking: Whence cometh he? who taketh us from the snare of this earthly tribulation? when cometh the time when we are released? behold we suffer long, enemies surround us, snares are set for our feet, we seek one who leadeth us unto the true God; earnestly we seek him and yet he cometh not; we hasten now his coming by inquiring of his identity.

Know ye, beloved, it hath been a goodly time since we listened to each other and said between ourselves: We make a great Bargain; we go into flesh; we seek to give mankind a sign that he cometh into a millennium if he but gives ear to the Voice of the Teacher.

It hath been a goodly time since we said, each unto the other: Let us all manifest in flesh again and see to it that humanity hath reason to know us by our works.

¶ I say unto you, beloved, our pact hath been kept. Ye have found yourselves in flesh. Ye have marveled that memory hath not been restored to you: ye have asked Me for memory. I say unto you it cometh in season. Grievously, I say, ye have been tormented by ignorance though ye winnowed the wheat from the chaff of experience and learned with cause to suspect whom ye are. So I say unto you more: the pact hath been twofold: First hath come the Mission. We are manifesting unto men that they may know they have their saviors, that the world is not a wilderness in which they are lost sheep, that we come to them with rejoicing, saying: Praise ye the Father! He hath sent us to minister to you!

That part of the pact was voluntary, I remind you. I said, Behold I go back to men in My flesh although it humbleth Me; I descend into physical form though it paineth Me.

Ye did say: Let us but go with Thee, Master, thus cometh a privilege.

I said: Go ye through into the world of flesh and I come after you by different means, using phenomena to accomplish that which men behold with their eyes.

Now do we approach the time of that seeing.

That part of the pact was one-fold; the second now approacheth, and men feel its imminence.

Lo, men shall be perplexed; the earth shall run mad; multitudes shall pass to and fro shouting of their terrors. They shall cry—

"A MONSTER MIRACLE HATH BEEN DONE! CHRIST THE LORD HATH BEEN SEEN! CAME HE IN A HIGH PLACE, BEHELD BY ALL WHO MET IN A CONFERENCE! RAISED HE HIS HAND IN REBUKE AND DECLARED: 'PEACE AMONG THE NATIONS LEST TOTAL DESTRUCTION END THEM!'"

They cry with a loud cry. They seek explanation. They come unto My servants saying: "Appeared He not at your behest, in that ye did call upon His name? Explain Him or we slay you! Devils or angels, what tell we our children concerning you?"

I say unto you, beloved, the second part of the pact then cometh.

Ye do rise in contriteness, each in his place and station, and respond—

"Nations, hear us! We speak by ordination. Long have we known that this would come to pass. Long have we prepared for it. Long hath it been revealed to us that men would come to the place where it was necessary. We did make pact with Him whom ye have beheld with your eyes. We came into the earth to herald Him whom ye hath seen. Yea did we walk after Him and before Him and make this explanation. Hear our voices, we say to you, lest His wrath be poured upon you and your hearts know an anguish.

"We say unto you, put up your arms, cast away your implements of war, be circumspect of demeanor nation to nation, help with the funds thereof the afflicted, bind up the wounds of your enemies, make them your brethren!"

Thus say ye to the nations, and they hear you.

Yet some hear you not. They shall say: "Away with these charlatans who speak blasphemies unto us!"

I tell you they shall try to take away your lives in that

they fear you. They shall stalk you unawares. They shall come upon you and raise their hands against you, but ye shall go unscathed because of the armor that is about you.

A time cometh when men shall rend themselves in that they fear that which they have witnessed; verily they shall gash themselves, making lamentations. They shall say, "Lucifer is with us! . . Lucifer hath tempted us!"

I say unto you they shall come upon a mountain and pray that they be delivered of his toils.

Behold, beloved, they ARE delivered, in that they hear your voices explaining it.

I say unto you the second part of the pact is simple yet difficult, in that it requireth stamina to endure. Ye are made of earthly clay in your bodies, knowing nerves and sinews that weaken under stress of danger.

Except ye be calm and great of faith, verily ye weaken truly. Ye do have spirit and it exalteth flesh: ye do have an errand to perform and it giveth you strength.

Upon another night I speak of it.

Thirteen is the Number.

Seven times seven is the Number of Days.

Mark these words well.

Hear ye My counsel and prepare to be wise in it . .

DIVINE DRAMA

DIVINE DRAMA

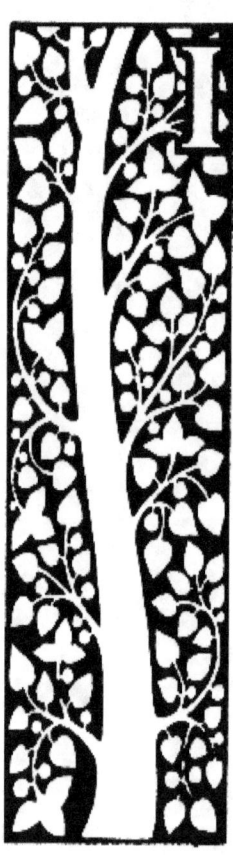

IT HAS been twenty-two years since that evening in West 51st Street when Mary brought her lap-board across to the divan on which I sat to give me my initiation in clairaudient recording. On the shelves of my library in Indiana of the present stand ten volumes of typed manuscripts, five hundred pages to the volume, containing the text communicated to me over more than two decades. Figuring three hundred words to the page, that totals a million and a half words covering every phase of eschatology that inquiring mind could ponder. To regurgitate all this wisdom out of Subconscious Mind would mean either reading books that have never been written, or vaingloriously crediting myself as the wisest man ever to be born—which of course I am not. The only sensible conclusion I have been able to draw, rationalizing the origin of such text, was said before me by the great astronomer Flammarion in the statement I previously quoted: "There exists in Nature, in myriad activity, a psychic element, the essential nature of which is still hidden to us." In other words, there must be such a thing as Invisible Intelligence that communicates itself by divers means and instruments into our visible world from an external source, and the text resulting—when recorded—is proof of it. Invisible Intelligence, however, postulates invisible life. The moment we entertain credence of invisible life we are entering a zone that Religion has ever commanded for its own. I could not have begun serious exploration of psychics without adventuring upon areas of religious jurisdiction. That I should proceed to encounter, so to speak, the ineffable personality of the Elder Brother, has been too profoundly private an enterprise for me to treat with crassly in a secular book. You will have noticed, perhaps, that I have included no descriptions of it in these pages—only the philosophy transmitted

What I now have to say by way of comment upon the whole of it is the unanswerable illation that I have satisfied my own heart that conscious life continues even though the body be destroyed, that this is not the first time my personality has been in mortal life and probably will not be the last, that there are transcendent beings in Cosmos who exercise daily influence on the comings and goings of men, that there is an Ancient of Days in command of our solar system whether or not He bothers himself about how many sparrows fall in any given day, that the Man of Galilee designated as His Son is neither Sabbath School myth nor bloodless statue in a church niche but a Splendorful Personality still concerned in His ministry—last but not least, that there are few inconsistencies or fantasies in Holy Writ when correctly interpreted. In short, human life to me has had most of the mystery and futility taken out of it, and with the uncertainties departed, plaguing the average individual, Peace of Mind has come in,

I am not unduly exercised by any experience which life may allot to me—so long as I feel the assurance that it is included in the program that determines my cosmic destiny ⚜

Having gone through this myself, having had implanted in my subconscious mind indeed—and with a vengeance—the transcendent interpretations I have been twenty-two years recording, I can only make compensation by passing it along in honest form to the harassed brother or sister who has not been so favored. I would be incurring the worst possible type of karmic debt, I am certain, if I did not do this. As industriously as I can, in my sunset years, I am recording and publishing the sixteen books of the Soulcraft Doctrine—of which this is fourth. Every mystery or complication which human life holds, somewhere has explanation or elucidation within these sixteen volumes. But the drama of the redemption of man is the greatest and most basic of them all. In "Behold Life" we had the general preview of why life functions and achieves in mortal form. In "Thinking Alive" we considered most of the vitalities of Thought as a creative and motivating universality. In "Earth Comes" we had the exposition of the integration of Cosmos and the solar planet on which we find ourselves in particular. In "Star Guests" we have the first broad foundations laid for the drama of Man as a creature of physical predicament and sensation—that has to be more minutely examined and assimilated in "Adam Awakes" . .

We as spiritual creatures do not belong to this planet, apparently. When the psalmist sang of man as being created "a little lower than the angels" he made a better designation than he realized. We are denizens of Cosmos, come from distant star worlds mightier than anything we now have in our horizons.

We are working out a Plan and a Pattern, and when we shall have it worked out fully we shall find ourselves back in the wondrousness of our once-discarded heritage but enhanced and exalted by the curriculum of our experiences. Meanwhile Death can hold no terrors for us, and the forces of evil can wreck only our bodies. There are whole phalanxes of new bodies up the coming centuries, waiting to enhouse and serve us. There can be no such thing as permanent separation from those we have loved, who have gone a little way in advance of us for the moment, but whom we must rejoin and travel with gloriously up the Golden Journey to a "heaven" beyond depiction. More than all else, the Teacher has assured us that every last one of us who desires it shall complete that Journey, that all are of equal rank upon it, that there are no outcasts and no lost ones.

We have survival, and adventure, and emotional and spiritual riches, and compassion, and help, and camaraderie, and reward assured to us. For what?

I say for nothing more than endeavoring insofar as mortal flesh allows us, to pattern our lives on the life of the Elder Brother and becoming as near like Him as we can.

¶ Peace of Mind?

Verily!

Dare to be yourself, and live the life you have chosen for yourself. That is the law and the prophets—for the enlightened ☆

But know why you are living it, and what lies at the end of it. Any professional police detective will tell you that when he has gathered all the evidence in a case, and every part fits into every other part, and every clue dovetails with every other clue, he knows beyond question he has found correct solution. When every part of this celestial doctrine fits every other part, and every shred of evidence about life up the worlds dovetails into every other shred of evidence and there are neither contradictions nor discrepancies, we should rest content in the logic we have found a true doctrine worthy of our endorsement. But we are promoting nothing theological or sectarian by what is disclosed that we relay to humanity. We say, these things we have found good and profitable and rational and satisfying to consider. Do you consider them with us, and if sobeit you arrive at our convictions from pondering all our evidence, we share that peace of mind with you and rejoice we can have brought it to you. All of us, in the last analysis, are but fellow and sister actors in a Divine Drama—the Drama of the Aeons.

We are to play our roles like the celestial performers that we are. And that is as far as we are committed to go with preaching . .

HAT interplanetary travel by disembodied souls is a probability should strain no one's credulity beyond the most fundamental claims of the orthodox Christian faith. Millions of rational Christians subscribe without difficulty to the tenet that when the body dies and the soul vacates it, the latter goes "up" to heaven; that Christ arose the third day after His crucifixion and "ascended" to some location that was concerned in altitude; that the Lord God came "down" and sought

out Adam and Eve in the cool of the evening in the Garden of Eden. Modern science, from astronomy to electronics—with radio and radar—has opened the upper ethereal regions to us and reasonably attested there is nothing of material substantiality above us that could pass as a literal heaven. Furthermore, we are forever called to remember that upon a rotating planet, what is "up" at this moment—in respect to our location—must be "down" twelve hours hence, unless the whole bag and baggage of the orthodox heaven whirls about us on the earth's atmospheric perimeter. And jet planes and stratospheric bombers would be bound to find some vestiges of it, if it did have substantiality, at the present acceleration of aeronautics.

Is the whole proposition not more reasonable to conceive when we visualize some other vast orb in the galactic system as being the Seat of the Godhead, and surviving personality finding post mortem means of leaving for it, and reaching it, and even coming back on occasion from it? Already our scientists are talking about interplanetary rocket travel. Couldn't discarnate thought succeed in performing what jet-driven rockets of materials may succeed in performing before the full story of "aviation" is recorded? The challenge is not illogical.

Somewhere in my psychical research writings I have told of the experiment of three mediumistic persons sitting in three different cities—New York, Boston, and

Niagara Falls—precisely at 9 p. m. of the same evening, and a discarnate personality going from one to the other in an almost instantaneous cycle, reading six words of a communication to each in successive fragmentary form, so that when the three came together and compared their fragments, putting them in chronological order, a unified and coherent message was assembled. If a discarnate mind can travel instantly from New York to Boston to Niagara Falls with sections of a uniform message in a few seconds of time, giving the effect of addressing three different persons in three different rooms with only a wall between them, why should not discarnate intelligence move from planet to planet, or heavenly body to heavenly body, with equal speed and facility, since distance can obviously be annihilated and made as naught by Thought?

It taxes the human intellect to its utmost, of course, to think of a great concourse of bodiless spirits journeying through interstellar space, discovering the earth-planet with all the zest of Columbus discovering the Americas, settling down upon it, and proceeding to prank biologically with the forms of sentient life indigenous to it. It taxes the intellect not from the premise that such an event happened or didn't happen, so much as from the realization of the stupendous astronomical distances that would have to be traversed to make it actual.

Nothing we know of, in Cosmos, surpasses the speed of

light—186,270 miles per second. Therefore in a year it travels 186,270 times 60 seconds a minute times 60 minutes an hour times 24 hours a day times 365.24 days a year, or 5,878,000,000,000 or nearly six trillion miles. When we attempt to realize that last night's light from Betelgeuse has been journeying to us at such speeds ever since the Dutch were paying $24 to the Indians for Manhattan Island, we may grasp some idea of how very far from us Betelgeuse is, seeing that the radiance from Betelgeuse only reached us last night after having been on its continuous celestial journey since 1655. And what goes for Betelgeuse goes for most of the stars in any evening's firmament.

Each has plenty of room to itself!

A mile, of course, is a comparatively small distance of measurement, brought down to the understanding of our physical bodies and finite minds. Still, it does give us a concept of distance to be covered. Space is so tremendous between the heavenly bodies that, as most schoolchildren know, astronomers have adopted a measuring system that represents the distance light can travel in a year, 5,878,000,000,000 miles or thereabouts. That represents One Light Year. It has taken at least 295 light-years for the radiance of Betelgeuse to reach us. Alpha Centauri is the nearest star-neighbor we possess in all the heavens, and the distance is 275,000 times the mileage from here to the sun—92 millions of miles—making Alpha Centauri a mere 275,400,000,000 miles away—practically just around the celestial corner. Grasp it if you can!

Respecting Sirius and its admittedly stupendous satellite, these are nearly 1,000,000 times as far away from us as our sun, or 92,000,000,000,000 earth-miles. This would mean that it is about one and a half light-years from us—another case of a heavenly orb just around the celestial corner as compared to Polaris or the Pleiades—that the brilliance that reached us from Sirius last night, started from it somewhere in the middle of 1941, this chapter being written of a spring morning in 1950.

Granted, therefore, that Thought could travel with the speed of light, or that discarnate souls started on a sojourn from the vicinity of Sirius and adventured toward the sun, finding our earth as one of its planets, would eight years and a half in the celestial area represent any formidable time-barrier for the trip? Furthermore, they mightn't—in all seriousness—have come here directly. They might have made planetary calls en route.

What I am bringing to your attention is the concept that none of this Migration Idea is materially preposterous. In fact, I can't see it as one-tenth as preposterous as essaying to locate "heaven" as just a few miles above our earthly heads. On the other hand, I CAN see every rationality and material credence in a "heaven" located on some gigantic orb afar in the galactic system, where the forms of developed conscious life are so much advanced over ours as to seem by comparison paradisical and angelic. Heaven of the Biblical presentation is only heaven anyhow through contrast with conditions on this earth as we know them.

THESE, admittedly, are big subjects but not quite so sizable as to be beyond analyzing. Space taken of and by itself is non-understandable. Always it must be attended with at least two points to mark it, whether they be dots on a drawingboard or suns in universal ether. And always remember that anything is "big", or any distance is "far", only as both are measured by our own physical infinitesimality. If each of us was large enough in corporal size to make a stride of 92,000-000 miles, Sirius would be only eight million paces from us, or a foot journey—judged by our present proportions—of slightly less than 1000 miles. If a person of present proportions walks four miles an hour, he can make such a trip in a little more than ten days.

It is therefore because we are so small physically, that Sirius seems such a tremendous distance from us. Thousands of men have been known to walk two to five miles twice a day, going to and from work, especially in our rural districts. Think what an unbelievable performance the same thing would be to a common garden variety of red ant.

Again and again we come back in all this, to the annoyance and irony of our microscopic organic size. What has it all to do with the Thought in our minds, that can traverse 92,000,000 miles to the sun in an instant of thinking? We say we can "imagine" ourselves in the igneous perimeter of the sun, although we may not be there personally, thank God, because if we were, we certainly wouldn't exist for any time to engage in thinking or anything else. Thought, I remind you, can "place" itself anywhere in a twinkling. And what right have we to say, considering such apparent fact, that disembodied souls—or souls no longer encumbered by organic bodies—can't "place" themselves anywhere in the galactic universe "in a twinkling"? We want to be cautious about denying it, lest all of a sudden we find ourselves doing it!

However, my purpose in compiling this volume has been specifically to bring these profundities to your attention. How far you wish to explore in them, how much additional knowledge you elect to acquire about them, is a matter of your concern privately. In the next volume, "Adam Awakes", we shall pick up the Sirian Migration anew and go further into the details of man discovering himself within an organic enhousement that proceeds to wear out and exhaust itself every seventy to ninety years, and what his manner has been in treating with it.

One thing is certain: Having once opened these appalling and entrancing topics to our view, and having gotten the fundamentals of them into our minds, there is little going back to our former provincial concepts.

Adults uniformly find no satisfaction in returning to their kindergarten classes of school days and learning how to sing one-verse songs and weave yarns of brilliant colors, accepting it as "education" . . not if they are adults mentally normal.

Having impregnated wisdom about this past Divine Drama in your Subconscious Mind therefore, where it can never be erased because nothing ever read into the Subconscious ever ceases to exist entirely, let me close this Volume Four on Soulcraft temporarily with a communication that I recorded on September 6, 1929—twenty-one years ago—that seems to have vital bearing on the international situation of today. Incidentally, it happens to be the perfect recapitulation of much of the Mystical History in this volume, with several points added not previously mentioned. It seemed to have been dictated by the same Sages of the Wisdom who gave Mary and myself our first clairaudient instruction. I close this volume with it—and the appropriate Benediction—

Human Destiny

DEAR BRETHREN IN MORTALITY:

EVERY age has its fresh revelation of man's history and destiny on this planet which he inhabits. Because of the times in which you live, revelations of a peculiar character have been disclosed to you in yours. Destiny forsooth, is a fearsome word—more fearsome than history. In history you know what has happened and can comprehend the worst. In destiny you have all the future sufferings and attainments of your species implied, and not always being able to comprehend them, you depict them in your intellects in terms of catastrophes. But be consoled in this: You live in a world of profit and purpose, and whosoever tells you otherwise is the enemy of your spirits. You are alive on earth to work out a program. You know profit as you live it. But you can best interpret what your destinies are to be by knowing the truth of what has happened in the past. And this we have sought to give you. Let us recapitulate, that for the years immediately ahead you may interpret events with intelligence—

Long ages ago it was decreed that man should meet with mishap. That is to say, the forces of ignorance and mischief too often called "evil" had gained such ascendancy over the race that man as Man was losing his identity. Bestialities and abominations, the crossings of immortal man's spirits with gross animalistic forms, were producing a race of hybrids so terrible that something had to be done to end it. The work of cleansing mankind was well-nigh imponderable of execution. Thought-forms were crossing with evolutionary forms; animals and men were becoming interchangeable. There were divine animals and beastly divinities. The whole sum and substance of life was a colossal abortion, serving no practical purpose, celestial or mundane. Each species could be sterilized, but that would mean cessation of propagation. Forms were already in existence that could manufacture offspring by other means than ovarian gestation. It was a horrible confusion, discouraging of solution.

Into this turmoil of insufferable satanities were called Radiant Beings from another system of creation. This creation had gone through the same—or a similar—experience-evolution in another world order, trillions of years before. They were popularly conceived of as super-angels. That is, they had been created of what we might consider angelic substance but in such form that they manifested differently than angels visiting earth commonly as messengers or guardians.

These Beings came to earth from other planets in other world systems, 144,000 of them, under a Leader whom men call Christ. He was leader of them because furtherest advanced in wisdom, compassion, understanding, and general character-nobility.

They came to earth in the midst of confusions, in a civilization far advanced over what humankind knows today. They were professors of divine secrets as to the literal construction of substance in Matter. They also possessed every other attribute of divine thought that can manifest on any level of physical existence.

They knew the secrets of earth and air and the compounds thereof. They took fleshly form for the same reasons that you have taken fleshly form in this generation: as supernal instructors. They founded a special tribe or family known as the Sons of Light in every language ☥

THE IDEA at first was to try to ameliorate the dastardly conditions they found, by inbreeding and improving a clean pure stock on a race of hybrids and intellectual blackguards. They were those who brought the Language of Thought among them, having the essence of every tongue in it. They were Radiant Beings in the word's fullest sense, intellectually, culturally, inventively, ethically, compassionately, constructively. They were the Super-Ministers to the universe. They came upon the earth to save it from itself, but quickly they perceived it was going to be impossible.

Thought had gained such headway in creation, that the

moment the correct amount of malice was generated, the world nearly exploded.

Malice or evil is a potential Force for Destruction that disintegrates matter even as Love propagates matter. When the point had been reached that Divine Love was superceded by Incarnate Evil—or destructive thought—the physical world wobbled, and it wobbles today. There might have been a solar catastrophe but for one thing: the Sons of Light saved it partially. That is to say, they deployed throughout the earth and balanced the forces of Destructive Evil with Constructive Love.

¶ These forces opposed one another for almost a million years, or thereabout, in earthly time. But the process was futile to this extent—

Those portions of earth into which they went, they preserved; those portions, or areas, where the blackness of intellect outdid the brightness, were destroyed by their own malevolence—a thing capable of happening again if mankind takes not warning. We are not of the opinion that it will happen, however, for the constructive Love Forces are again in the ascendant.

These forces of evil, however, knowing the end of their reign was approaching, made caskets of cement wherein they entombed the secrets of their culture, thinking to perpetuate it in event they reincarnated. But such reincarnation never came to pass. It was necessary for those secrets to be permanently destroyed, not in the sense of spirit disintegration but in a sense of intellect,

They were given positions of inferiority in the household of the planets—spiritually speaking—where they remain to this day, not writhing in any physical agony according to modern theologians but with their mischievous intellects numbed, so to speak, by what might be considered a form of supercilious humor, or outraged intellect, seeking expression in futility.

That is to say, these beings were removed from the earth-sphere and taken back to the planets from which they originally came, but marked with a sign on their foreheads, not a literal sign but a "numbness of intellect" that seeks expression in forms of supercilious humor that makes them treat the earth creation as a sort of divine jest, seeing no seriousness in it. The "devil" so-called, or Beelzebub, or Lucifer if you prefer, was one of those with the greatest sense of diabolic humor. Not that humor is diabolic. It is the healthiest attribute which man possesses, but in fiendish form it is intellect gone to seed.

THIS MISCHIEF-PLAGUE was therefore removed from among the antediluvian nations but only by the catastrophe that is known allegorically as the Fall of the Angels. You perceive now, we think, where the Biblical legend came from. It is in every race and culture in some aspect, because every race and culture had in it the Beelzebubian heritage in the survivors of catastrophe. Now then, take this—

The Master of the Host appeared first on earth as a man, and set up a dynasty that ruled for interminable generations, giving the race its first notions of kingship. When He saw how matters were proceeding in consultation with His viceroys and lieutenants of similar origin, He decided the earth must be purged of abominations. Succeeding in the transfer of the Dark People elsewhere, which of course extended throughout the earth as the earth was then known, He gathered together His band and took them to a location that now approximates Egypt and Transjordania on this planet.

The last Flood came and caught them, apparently drowning them physically with the rest. But that was expected and provided for. Physical death meant nothing to Sons of Light. The legend of Noah is symbolic of a great condition which maintained among certain other followers who rode the face of the waters to keep a clean species in physical preservation until the waters subsided.

The legend of Noah taking pairs of animals into the Ark is nowhere authenticated. There seems to be no record of this in any higher reaches of Time and Space, excepting as men have tried to account for the preservation of animal species from time to time, not knowing that all parts of the planet were not submerged. A careful check was made and clean species allocated to certain positions that would not be affected.

There is only so much water in the mundane universe

and how it is distributed is relatively unimportant. If the land sank in one portion of the globe and was covered by water, dry areas were left elsewhere that had been thus uncovered.

Now then, when the last Flood came, man was caught on the horns of a dilemma, so to speak. He had, by his own malfeasance, precipitated the cataclysm. He had spurned the goodly counsel of the 144,000. He thought for a time to preserve his culture by burying it in such form that it could later be unearthed. But nothing so happened. The "magicians" in the main were exiled. The rest were allowed to keep their earthly residence under terms of self-castigation. That is, they discerned the folly in what they had done and repented. But they could not always get rid of their animal natures by which they have been plagued since in physical manifestation ⚹

Know therefore that when they came to the point of realizing their malfeasance, they were lectured and permitted to remain on this planet under sufferance, that thereafter they would employ their diabolical talents constructively. Thus do we get a race of so-called Scientists functioning upon this earth in the present order. They are, by and large, the souls of the old repentant magicians, pledged to do goodly work under pain of banishment, and slowly working out their destinies by mechanistic forms and enchantments of inventions.

Man as man, however, had deteriorated so far that only

through untold millennia, and much instruction, could he win back to his former standards of intelligence. When the catastrophe was over, he began reincarnating according to the direction of the 144,000, in the form which the Host Itself had employed: a sort of sublimated ape, or physical man as you know him today, slowly, slowly working his way up through the aeons and still working it. Now we are going to tell you something you do not know—

MAN as man is a creature spiritually compounded but ethically projected into a world of Cause and Effect to work back toward his former state but minus his capacity for destructive mischiefs. More than that, the essential part of the Plan is this: He has inherent in his spiritual nature much of his lost heritage but is forbidden by Thought Forces superior to him to use it until he has reached that time when he is so spiritually balanced and developed that he will never again employ his knowledge selfishly or malevolently. But that time is far closer to hand than men generally suppose.
It is so close, we tell you, that a curious condition has arisen in men's affairs.
Spirits that have no business on earth, that never had any part in the former malevolence, that do not belong to this earth-system and cannot possibly benefit by anything it has to offer, have gotten into the earthly scheme despite all that the Host and the Sons of Light have been

able to do, and have enlightened humankind before it is healthily ready to be enlightened.

Understand, they have not meant to be malicious. They have even tried to aid, but they have precipitated a condition of affairs where drastic means are necessary to accelerate man's spiritual nature in order that he may not use this uninvited enlightenment in a sort of ignorant malice toward himself.

These "foreign spirits" belong to an order that would not be intelligible to you. They are great knaves in one respect: that they have meddled, and are meddling, where they have no business. They have besieged statesmen in the main, and worked politically after a fashion, to bring about a millennium of their own, irrespective of man's present incapacity to live under it. These spirits began to operate, we tell you, about a hundred years back in your solar time, motivating the soul called Napoleon to imitate the Caesars. Their latest motivation has been the leaders of Russia.

Understand, they are not bad people but simply meddlers—and too frequently muddlers—amusing themselves after a fashion with a type of mischief they think creditable. Frequently they incarnate themselves as leaders ahead of their times. Lenin was one of these, and there may be others yet to be reckoned with, for they are fully as powerful as any of us and the Master feels it His province not to combat them but rather to outwit them by a superior play of intelligence and love.

NOW YOU see exactly what is going on in this world and where we come in. Scores of you now in flesh, identifying yourselves as the Master's compatriots in this great work of redemption—the REAL redemption —had not meant to incarnate in this generation after what you had done in lives lived since Galilee, but it was plain to be seen that superior leadership was necessary to steer awakening mankind around the pitfalls of immature knowledge. So scores of you volunteered to take no rest, but to go immediately back into earth-life and assume the burden of a general social counseling that should hold the body politic together if the countries of the earth went into mad panic at what easily might be revealed ahead of society's capacity to interpret it

The Master has said that He would do something that He has never done since antediluvian days. With the help of the Host whose concentrated thought would supply the necessary power, He would show Himself to the nations at the psychological moment when mankind in general was about to run amok and commit military excesses as of a child crazed by fear.

He agreed with the rest of the group to make Himself visible when the proper time should come—and if it should come—that His literal presence would have the effect of bringing such panic to a merciful stabilization. This panic could easily be brought about by a coalition of oriental nations—of which Russia is leader—gaining such ascendancy that they threaten to overrun and subjugate the globe, reducing its white and Christian peoples to bondage. All the mightiest instruments of bloodshed and extermination that could be manufactured would be brought into play and used to coerce a mad world that lies seemingly powerless before such onslaught ✡

These are the problems—and the Problem—that we of the Sons of Light have to contend with, in this generation ✡

We are proceeding boldly with its solution in these vital months and hours, increasing all our forces, calling on all loyal lovers of the Christ to aid and dispatch this most exquisite of all brevets.

Understand this mission. Take it to heart. Comparatively few of earth's millions know the true essence of the Christian religion. To those of you who have been vouchsafed the light, we say unto you: SPREAD IT!
¶ Tell men that Jesus the Christ is a Reality.

Tell them He lives and reigns even now.

Thus shall a great peace visit you, which is your reward for this service. You shall know the Benediction that is our benediction nightly: Well done, thou good and faithful servant; enter thou into the joy of thy Lord! . .

.. *BENEDICTION* ..

MY DEAR ONES:

BE ASSURED I am with you. This is My word to you: Be calmer and happier. Each morning is beautiful. Each day is bright with promise. Be truer in your hearts to the world that is about you. Do not cohabit with the Enemy in your minds.

Ye are of the flesh and yet not of it. Ye are made mortal for a mission. That mission is the interpretation of the Great Drama of Earth and Time, which endeth with the Miracle of which you have been enlightened.

It is an equally great mission inasmuch as it requireth great travail of spirit before mankind is brought to recognize its significance.

Not in a moment, nor yet in a year, will the world accept that I live and reign. Men will scoff as of old; men will doubt as of old; men will break faith as of old; the Enemy will capitalize the phenomenon among the illiterate; he will make vast numbers believe that the devil hath wrought a piece of play-acting for his purpose.

I say, keep strong in the knowledge of our kinship. Keep strong in your fortitude that the Son of Man is the Prince of Earth, that ye are His emissaries. Let not your hearts be troubled. Cometh a day of beautiful reward that ye have so served. There are those who discredit you already for My sake. There are those who love and admire you already for My sake. The last are My sheep. Feed them well. Fear not to reward them with that which Holy Spirit prompteth you to feed them ☧

When ye do speak, all of you, let your words be yea, yea, and nay, nay. Let our hearts be judges of our tongues. Men will see your good works and your words shall be borne on the wings of achievements.

Fear not to tell of personal reactions to Me. Know that in such times I do come close and listen with a gratitude. For this were ye, My servants, sent into the world in this generation.

No matter whether ye do bear testimony of Me unto the millions or to the one, they are My sheep whom ye feed, and My love and My benediction and My blessing and heart's gratitude goeth with your speech.

Know that ye are not sent unto a country but unto a world. Ye have been born into flesh in order to know the advantage of life in a nation that is the world's leader among all older nations, in attestment of Me.

Ye have been born of humble parents, most of you, that ye might know the joys of humble pastimes and the sor-

rows of humble livings. I too chose humble parents ☙
Ye have come the long and tortuous road to greet each other. Know that ye are whom ye are: it was part of the covenant. Had ye known otherwise ye would not have reacted as normal men and women. Know that ye did go through childhood, youth, and early maturity having earthly vicissitude for similar reason. Ye were called many times to strange vicissitudes that ye could not interpret by worldly standards. Ye were watched and guarded by My servants from your births into flesh.
¶ So it hath ever been till the cycle now closeth and ye know whom ye are.
Let yourselves be at peace.
Increasingly shall ye realize that ye are my literal husbandmen and husbandwomen. It shall be your shield and buckler, your shibboleth and insignia, your passport and your transport. Be of calm joy and loving toleration for all earthly creatures whom ye resemble: they have their heights to scale, even as ye are scaling yours to find Me at the summit.
Now, My beloved, the world calleth: the day groweth strong: the business of life demandeth us. Rest secure in My assertion that even the least of you is supported by the Everlasting Arms and that the work of interpreting Me to My world can never be other than a source of joyous gratification.
I am your prince: I am your Elder Brother: I am your servant. I come and go among those who love Me and

keep My adjurations. Store My words in your hearts. Keep My blessing in your souls. We travel for and do great labor for the approval of the Father. Help the sons of men. Save them from their follies. Turn their feet in the roads of light and their faces in the ways of wisdom. Verily they shall rise up in the Last Days and call you blessed, though they never know whom they blessed ✠
I leave you now with My words on your foreheads.

PEACE

FINIS

SO YOU ARRIVE AT THE END OF THE VOLUME NAMED STAR GUESTS THAT WAS WRITTEN AND INSPIRATIONALLY RECORDED FOR THE SOULCRAFT AUDIENCE AND DONE INTO A BOOK BY SOULCRAFT PRESS, AN INDIANA CORPORATION, WHOSE ADDRESS IN JUNE OF THE YEAR ONE THOUSAND NINE HUNDRED AND FIFTY IS NOBLESVILLE, A TOWN IN THE STATE OF INDIANA IN THE UNITED STATES OF AMERICA ✠ ✠

www.ingramcontent.com/pod-product-compliance
Lightning Source LLC
Chambersburg PA
CBHW050337230426
43663CB00010B/1894